D1524589

# Shocking Psychic Solution: The Lizzie Borden Case

## By Richard and Debbie Senate

*This report is a psychic inquiry and proposed solution to the unsolved Fall River murders of Andrew and Abby Borden, August 4, 1892*

GLOBAL COMMUNICATIONS / INNER LIGHT PUBLICATIONS

Formerly titled: **The Psychic Solution: The Lizzie Borden Case**,
Published in 1998 by the Phantom Bookshop.
Now with additional material composed and updated by the authors.

Nonfiction - Metaphysics

ISBN: 1-60611- 000- 4
EAN: 978-160611-000-3

Timothy Green Beckley, Editorial Director/Publisher
Carol Rodriguez, Publishers Assistant
Copy Editor, Sean Casteel

For free catalog write:
Global Communications
Box 753
New Brunswick, NJ 08903

For free subscription to Conspiracy Journal E mail Newsletter
www.ConspiracyJournal.com

Contact Rights Manager at MRUFO8@hotmail.com
for reprints and translation rights.

This book is dedicated to the Memory of
Gene Lee Noble
(1908—1983)
A man who always loved a good mystery.

The authors would like to thank the following people:
John Anthony Miller
Katie Crawford
Megan Senate
Shain Neumeier

# Table of Contents

# SHOCKING PSYCHIC SOLUTION:

# RICHARD AND DEBBIE SENATE

Debbie Senate is a well-respected psychic who has helped many people with her gifts, from police murder cases to lost pets. For many years she wrote an advice column titled "Dear Debbie" that used her psychic impressions to give answers to people's problems. She is a gifted medium as well as wife and mother of three. She resides now with her husband and daughter, Megan, in Oak View, California.

Richard Senate is best known as a ghost hunter and psychic researcher. For 22 years he was the historian for the city of Ventura and operated a historical museum. He has appeared on numerous TV and Radio shows as an expert on the paranormal. He is the author of 14 published books with his most recent being Hollywood Ghosts and The Ghosts of the California Missions. He began to research and investigate phantoms when he saw one himself in 1978. He still gives ghost tours of Ventura and contributes articles to magazines and newspapers. He can be reached at his website www.ghost-stalker.com .

Debbie Senate                    Richard Senate

# WHO IS RICHARD SENATE?

Richard Senate was born in Los Angeles, California. His father was a painter at MGM studios and worked on such classic films as "The Wizard of Oz." Richard's Family moved to Thousand Oaks in 1952 and he has been a resident of Ventura County for most of his life. He went to Ventura High School, Ventura Community College and Long Beach State University where he earned a degree in History.

He worked his way though school doing odd jobs and struggling, unable to buy books he needed (he checked out similar books from the library or borrowed copies).

He did a years post graduate work in Anthropology at UC Santa Barbara with plans to do archaeology. While at a field school held by Cal Poly San Luis Obispo, held at Mission San Antonio de Padua, he saw a ghost. The image was that of a monk. This chance encounter changed his whole life. He began to study ghosts and related supernatural topics becoming one of the pioneers in the study of the paranormal.

He has continued his work investigation from that time on. He has appeared on such TV shows at the "Search for Haunted Hollywood" (Fox) "Sightings" (UPN), "Haunted Houses" (A&E) "Haunted Hotels and Haunted History" (History Channel) Most recently he appeared on "DeadFamous " (UK). He is the author of 14 published works on ghosts and history including "Hollywood Ghosts", "Ghosts of the Haunted Coast" and "Ghost-stalker's Guide to Haunted California".

"Shocking Psychic Solution : The Lizzie Borden Case," (with Debbie Senate) is his newest work. He leads tours of haunted sites and holds classes on ghost hunting in Ventura, California. He also managed two historic museums as well as served the city of Ventura as a historian for 22 years.

He lived briefly in Carson City, Nevada where he investigated several haunted sites in that community and Virginia City. He writes a column in the Ojai Valley Voice newspaper of psychic subjects and contributes to the Ventura County Star newspaper (yourhub.com). He currently resides in Oak View, California, a small town of 5,000, seven miles north of Ventura with his wife of 24 years and their 17 year old daughter Megan. Richard continues to research and investigate the unknown seeking answers to the riddles of ghosts and haunted houses.

# SHOCKING PSYCHIC SOLUTION:

# INTRODUCTION:
# WHY DOES THE LIZZIE BORDEN CASE FASCINATE US?

It took place over a century ago. It was two obscure murders committed in a savage way yet they still enthrall the public imagination. Perhaps it is the fact that the crime is still unsolved that so haunts us still. Most believe that the daughter, Lizzie Borden, took the ax and did the savage crime but, if that is true, how did she do it? How did she hide the murder weapon and how did she manage to do the terrible act without getting covered in blood? What would cause a Sunday school teacher to snap in such a way as to do in her hated stepmother and elderly father? By all accounts, Andrew Borden loved his daughter and was generous to her in ways he was never generous to others. Witnesses confirmed Lizzie returned his love. No one could even imagine she would slay him. Her stepmother perhaps, her father, never.

The brutality of the attacks was enough to cause public shock, but few could imagine this was the act of a woman. It flew in the face of all Victorian logic that a frail woman would have the stealth and the rage to commit these bloody murders. Though the public knew there was little love between Lizzie and her stepmother, Abby, everyone knew how much her father doted on her; she seemed to have had a strong relationship with him.

When he died he was still wearing the ring she had presented to him on his little finger. What horrible thing had dislodged her love and sent her, if she did it, into such a killing frenzy? Like the awful murders of Jack the Ripper in London's Soho district two decades before, the Fall River murders stunned the public and challenged their Victorian standards.

# Shocking Psychic Solution:

The Borden Family was, in our modern terms, dysfunctional, and had been for the last five years. Like many blowups, it started small and built slowly. They were abnormal for their day. Andrew Borden could best be described as an American version of "Ebenezer Scrooge." Those who knew him described him as a cold, moneygrubber who saw the world only in terms of profit and loss. Upon learning of his passing most were pleased rather than saddened. He had few friends in Fall River among all classes.

His only human quality was his soft spot towards his daughters, Lizzie and her sister, Emma. Even his second wife hadn't won a secure place in his heart. When his first wife passed away, Andrew followed the tradition of the times and re-married. It was believed that children needed a mother to raise them and to manage the house. A new wife would provide stability to the family.

The problems in the family all started over money, that root of all evil. In a bid to make more money, Andrew "gave" a house to Abby, the second wife. It was all a well thought-out plan and one that he didn't share with his daughters. Somehow, the cat got out of the bag. Lizzie heard about the deal at church and was livid. To make up for the deal, Andrew gave Lizzie and Emma each a house—they could keep the rent on those houses as their personal income. He also treated Lizzie to an escorted trip to Europe. The grand tour was something young people did. Sometimes young women would find husbands on these long journeys that were both cultural and educational. The tour wasn't cheap and it is doubtful Andrew would have come forward with this "gift" if he hadn't deemed it necessary.

By all accounts, the trip didn't work out and the animosity lingered still. Lizzie stopped calling Abby "mother" and began referring to her simply as "Mrs. Borden." Before this they had gotten on rather well. Emma had never warmed to Abby. Abby was a hard person to like. In many ways she complimented Andrew. She, like her husband, had few friends, ran the house to his frugal tastes and did the cooking herself, reducing the need for a cook in the household. They got on with a single servant, an Irish girl.

Lizzie and the Irish servant seem, by all accounts, to have gotten along well, yet as the case progressed, it was this Irish girl who gave the most damming testimony against Lizzie. Then there was the break-in. The home was always kept locked in an era where this was almost unheard of. People of that day, rich or poor, almost never locked their doors.

And seeing as many people had a small arsenal of weapons in their homes, breaking in while people were on the premises was a hazardous undertaking. Yet the home was broken into months before the murders. A nail was found in the door lock as if to imply the door lock had been forced. Only a few items were taken.

This break-in had all the earmarks of the classic "inside job." Was this a set up for the killings? Or, could it have been real enough? Andrew, as a mean slumlord and loan shark, had many enemies. He and his family might well have been targets. To compound things, the house wasn't up to their social status. It was an old, shabby, former rental set up originally as a duplex. It was not in a good part of town either; far from "the Hill" where other members of the Borden's family resided in Victorian opulence. As Andrew and his family really didn't entertain (too expensive), the home's single grace was its location close to the downtown business district. Andrew could walk to work without the need of a horse and buggy (they had a barn for one but, outside of visits from their Uncle John who had a horse and buggy, it was unused, save for storage).

Which brings us to Uncle John V. Morse. He was one of the most mysterious characters in the sad drama. He dressed as shabbily as a tramp yet he was almost as rich as Andrew. He was the brother of Andrew's first wife and the daughters' uncle. He and Andrew seemed to get on well enough and one might even call them friends (if that name could be applied to any of Andrew's relationships). Andrew admired John's frugal nature. If anyone could pinch a nickel better than Andrew it was John. Together they had hatched the deal to buy a farm and put it in Abby's name. John didn't spill the beans about the deal until it was too late. Many have pointed out that John liked to stir things up.

If he hadn't had a good alibi, his neck would have most assuredly been in the noose. The detailed alibi was almost too perfect, as if it was meticulously constructed for some purpose. There are many questions linked to Uncle John, such as why he appeared unexpectedly the night before the murders. He spent the night at the house without a bag or change of clothes. It was while Abby was changing the sheets he had slept in that she was attacked and hacked to death with 14 blows from an ax-like weapon.

Another curious feature has to do with poison. Lizzie tried several times to purchase poison. Not just any poison, but virulent Prussic Acid. Poison was long thought to be the woman's weapon, but even in those times the serious nature of this poison was recognized and it couldn't be purchased over the counter. One needed a prescription. She told of needing the acid to refresh a skin cape—in the middle of summer. Why didn't she purchase the arsenic that would be had without a fuss? Prussic Acid was a popular poison for women who took their own lives. It is noted that Lizzie had a book on household hints. The section on poisons had been referred to so much the spine was broken in that section. To add to the confusion, Abby was paranoid she would be poisoned. She even saw a doctor in the belief she had been given a toxic drug. Why did Lizzie stick with the hard-to-get drug rather than do further research into other poisons one could find in any early Twentieth Century drug store? Or was this too some sort of setup for the murders? Had Abby died of poison, Lizzie would have been suspected and, in all likelihood, been convicted and sentenced to hang for the crime.

Other strange elements have come down from the court records that throw doubt onto Lizzie's seemingly open and shut guilt. People did see a strange coach near the house. One witness saw someone who seemed to deliver a note. People reported seeing Lizzie standing in the doorway of the barn at the suspected time of the murders.

Even in the face of many conflicting statements as to what she was doing and what had happened the day of the killings, she had supporters who believed she was innocent. The facts seem incontrovertible. Lizzie was in the house while Bridget was outside washing the windows at the time of the murder of Abby. She was in the house when her father was killed an hour and a half later. Still, with Andrew's many enemies, the strange things that happened, and all of the conflicting stories, it wasn't hard to spin a defense around reasonable doubt. Even if Lizzie did the terrible act, how did she do it and how did she keep her dress from being splattered with blood and gore? How had she hidden the murder weapon? It just didn't seem natural or even believable.

Lizzie was set free to live a life as an outcast, believed by society to be a murderess. She did her best to live a normal life, turning to her pets and having a relationship with another woman. But she was a woman scorned in polite society and mocked by children's rhymes. The house where the murders took place is now a bed and breakfast and many spending the night there tell of strange supernatural events, ghostly echoes of the crimes that took place in those rooms. Perhaps Lizzie haunts there still.

One last thought. If you believe Lizzie did slay her father and stepmother you must take into account the fact that doctors examining the bodies of the two victims believe the killer swinging the murder weapon was left handed. Lizzie Borden was right handed.

# SHOCKING PSYCHIC SOLUTION:

# THE PROLOGUE AND CAST OF CHARACTERS

On August 4, 1892, two people were murdered in their home with an axe. The crime has stimulated speculation, novels, books, a ballet and movies over the years. Lizzie Borden, the youngest daughter of the murdered man, was arrested for the crime and placed on trial. A jury of her peers (all men) found her not guilty but people have wondered for over a century if she was really responsible for the terrible murders. The facts in the case are deceptively simple and mirror every locked room mystery ever written. The family, uncharacteristically, kept their house locked because the father, Andrew Borden, was a wealthy slumlord and banker with many enemies in the town of Fall River, Massachusetts.

## The Cast of the Tragedy

The Victims:

1. **Abby Borden**: Age 68. Five feet tall, weight over 200 pounds. A serious, dour woman who almost never left the house. She had no friends; she was Andrew's second wife and took care of the home. She was hated by her stepdaughters, Emma and Lizzie, but the relationship between Lizzie and Abby was affectionate early on. She was discovered in the second floor guest room, next to the bed, with her head brutally hacked with some edged weapon like an axe. She had faced her attacker. She was the first to die that fateful day.

2. **Andrew Borden**: Age 70. Son of a fish peddler, he built a fortune as a slumlord, mill owner, and banker. He exploited his workers, evicted tenants, and charged usurious interest. His enemies were legion. He loved his two daughters and had a soft spot for Lizzie. All accounts record that she and her father had a good relationship and she seems to have loved her father. At the time of his death, he was worth about a half million dollars, a huge amount of money at that time.

The Suspects:

1. **Lizzie Borden**: Age 32. An active church worker. She lived with her father, sister, and stepmother.

   Motive: Hate. Her father had transferred property to her stepmother.

   Opportunity: She was in the house when both murders took place.

   Suspicious Circumstances: Lizzie tried to buy poison at a drug store. She claimed Abby had received a note calling her away. She was seen burning a stained dress.

   Tried for the crime and found innocent.

2. **Emma Borden**: Age 41. She also lived in the house.

   Motive: Inheritance of the estate. A longstanding hatred of Abby.

   Opportunity: None, as she was visiting friends in Fairhaven some fifteen miles away.

   Suspicious circumstances: A carriage was seen in the road to the house. Her alibi wasn't confirmed.

3. **John V. Morse:** The overnight houseguest. Andrew's brother-in-law from his first his first marriage, Lizzie and Emma's uncle.

Motive: None known, but he did oppose the transfer of real estate to Abby.

Opportunity: He had an airtight alibi for Andrew's murder, but not Abby's. His Alibi was good, almost too good.

4. **The Unknown Stranger**: A young man was seen loitering around the Borden house that morning by neighbors. He was seen over a period of hours. He looked like he was waiting for someone or something.

Motive: Andrew had many enemies in town.

Suspicious Circumstances: The doors were locked except for a short period of time at the Borden House.

## Shocking Psychic Solution:

# Timeline of the Fall River Murders

The murders took place two hours apart.

*9:00 am* Andrew Borden leaves for work. Abby seen dusting downstairs. Abby tells Bridget to wash the outside of the windows. Abby and Lizzie alone in the house.

*9:30 am* Abby Borden hacked to death in the upstairs guest bedroom.

*10:30 am* Andrew returns home sick. Lizzie tells him that Abby had gotten a note and left. Bridget feels ill and goes to her room upstairs. Lizzie and Andrew were alone in the downstairs of the house.

*11:30 am* Andrew Hacked to death as he slept on the horsehair sofa in the downstairs sitting room. Lizzie's screams call maid down stairs. The neighbors were alerted and they call Dr. Bowen. Lizzie claimed to have been in the barn at the time of the murders.

*12:00* Noon. Abby Borden's body found.

# Shocking Psychic Solution:

Andrew    Abby

# THE LIZZIE BORDEN MURDER CASE

History isn't a perfect tapestry. Being a thing fabricated by human beings, it is filled with oversights, omissions and downright lies. Some things become lost in the historic record because they were just forgotten or because they didn't fit into the established norms. The human animal hates the incompleteness of the unknown and seeks to fill in the gaps with theory and conjecture.

But there is another way to dispel the unknowns that just might give a new rationale to the classic mysteries of history. Time travel is beyond our known abilities and, lacking new observable evidence, many feel content with the existing record and the many theories propounded by so-called experts. Perhaps there is another way.

## Psychic Detection

Some people throughout history have possessed unique psychic gifts. The records of psychic research in the last hundred and twenty years are filled with accounts of gifted people solving crimes or finding missing children. There are even records of such gifted people speaking with the dead. Such conversations have turned up data they could not have known through normal means. Psychics and their accomplishments have been with mankind from the dawn of human history and they can be found in the earliest writings of Egypt, Babylon, China and India.

Is it possible that a gifted psychic could attempt to solve the greatest mysteries of the past? Could such a person part the veil of time and give new testimony in cases believed to be insoluble? The evidence collected by such "psychic sleuthing" might not be admissible in a court of law, but it might give closure needed to answer doubts and speculations.

Such activity is within the domain of what is called today "psychic detective work" and "psychic archaeology." It is a branch of psychic research and parapsychology. To test this theory, the Lizzie Borden Project was started. An older case was selected to avoid libel laws or any chance that a guilty party might escape justice by saying a jury was influenced by a psychic. The Fall River Tragedy was ideal to the experiment as it is well known and well documented. No one involved is alive today so no one will be harmed by the findings of the psychic.

The results of this test can in no way be weighed as solid evidence but it might serve to open new lines of investigation in the case that could lead to a solution. Read this study and see what you think.

# The Lizzie Borden Case

Psychometric tests were used in this investigation—the target items from the Lizzie Borden House and grounds as well as pictures taken of the individuals involved and the death scenes. The house is now open as a Bed and Breakfast. Spend the night there where others have seen ghosts and see if you come up with another solution.

# Shocking Psychic Solution:

# THE REMOTE VIEWER:
# DEBBIE CHRISTENSON SENATE

Debbie Christenson Senate first realized she was different from other children when she was six. She just "knew things" that others didn't. It was in a park that she first had an experience that caused her parents to take notice. She was approached by an old woman in strange clothing. She talked of butterfly wings and other things. Her parents saw their daughter talking to thin air and went to her only to be repulsed by an ear-piercing buzz. Later Debbie saw a picture of the woman in an old album. She was a great grandmother Debbie never met from Sweden. Her parents were tolerant of her unusual ability but advised her to keep her psychic side well hidden from classmates and members of her church (LDS).

Still she saw things in her mind's eye. School was easy as the answers just came to her almost automatically. She was in her twenties when she first unfolded as a psychic and she began to use her many psychic talents to help others. These included people she knew and people she did not know. On several occasions she assisted local law enforcement in finding solutions to baffling murder cases.

When asked to take part in this experiment in psychic detective work she was willing and eager. She had long been interested in the Lizzie Borden Case and thought it would make an ideal test for this new way of looking at history's mysteries. She couldn't guarantee a solution, but she was willing to try. Several attempts were made in the next three weeks. The last attempt gained the most answers. The findings were not what we expected.

If the impressions are correct Lizzie didn't do it! You might be surprised to discover who did.

THE LIZZIE BORDEN CASE

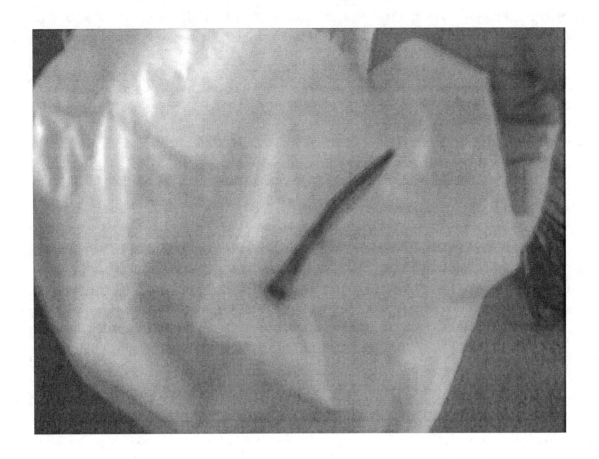

# SESSION NUMBER ONE
# THE NAIL FROM THE BACK PORCH

One of the oldest forms of psychic gifts is that of psychometry, that is, feeling objects and using psychic impressions to gain some insights on the object and its owner. Debbie has been an accomplished psychometrist for many years and has baffled non-believers with her ability to use personal items to give detailed readings of past events. Could this ability bridge the gap in both time and space and give a new testimony to the riddle of the Fall

# SHOCKING PSYCHIC SOLUTION:

Rivers Murders?  I was convinced that such an experiment was worth the effort.  But for Debbie to pick up on anything or even focus upon a given place she must have an object, something physical, to touch and hold.  This would act as a sort of psychic anchor that would enable her to transcend time and, perhaps, see the truth in this unique case.

Fortunately, we have a friend who lives not far from Fall River and was able to visit the place where the killings took lace and secure some artifacts from the owners.

The home is now converted into a bed and breakfast inn.  Many come from far and wide to spend a night in the old house to gain their own insights to the case. Wendy S., our friend, managed to secure a single nail from the back porch.  It was removed when the home was recently remodeled. The nail was carefully wrapped and sent to California. The new owners were excited about the project and were helpful.  Once it arrived, the nail was placed in the study under lock and key. At no time was Debbie permitted to see or hold the piece.  We wanted her first impressions recorded fresh.  As in all psychic research, there is an element of danger. We are dealing with the unknown and when walking in an uncharted domain one must be wary.  We started with a period of meditation and relaxed imagery. Then, the lights were dimmed and soft music played to help keep the relaxed mood.  Debbie rested on a number of pillows, stretched out on the bed. Her eyes were closed. I asked if she thought she was ready and when she nodded, I turned on the tape recorder and gave her the nail. I made sure I didn't touch it with my own hands keeping it in its tissue paper. She rolled it over in her hands once, then twice. With her eyes still closed, I noticed her face change from a look of total peace to one of pain and curiosity. What follows is a transcription of that session, as it was recorded by the tape recorder:

Debbie: "I see a pear tree, it is a very small pear tree but I see fruit upon it."

# THE LIZZIE BORDEN CASE

Richard: "Do you see anyone?"

Debbie: "Yes, I see water on the ground, soapy water."

Richard: "Do you see someone?"

Debbie: "Yes, It's a woman. She is hot, so very hot today. She dips a rag in the bucket and holds it to her neck. She is confused by something. Something isn't right. She feels sick."

Richard: "How sick?"

Debbie: "Her stomach, it is the summer sickness. She would have gone except for that... (Could not hear tape) that and the Mrs."

Richard: "What Mrs.?"

Debbie: "The mistress of the house, Mrs. Borden. She told her to wash the windows and that's what she would do. Besides it was better than staying indoors on a day like today. And there was the pear tree. The pears would make her stomach feel better."

Richard: "Did she eat the pears?"

Debbie: "Yes, she took her time too."

Richard: "Is she the servant girl Bridget?"

Debbie: "They call her Maggie. She hates that, but there is something that keeps her here. She likes the Mrs. And this place would be like any other. This place isn't an easy place but an Irish girl could do a lot worse."

Richard: "Does she long to go home to Ireland?"

Debbie: "Not particularly. She has family but she likes America and all its wide-open spaces. She has dreams too, you know."

## SHOCKING PSYCHIC SOLUTION:

Richard: (pause) "Is there anyone else there?"

Debbie: "She saw him today; he had a dark look about him too. He's young but no good. There is a dark cloud about the fellow." (Debbie's voice took on an Irish lilt)

Richard: "Who? Was it Mr. Andrew Borden?"

Debbie: "No, the other man, the stranger, the dark stranger. Sure nothin' good can come from the likes of such as him. There is the look of the gallows all about him. She is scared of his kind. She has seen them before in the old place."

Richard: "Then, this man she saw was a stranger? What was he doing?"

Debbie: "Looking, just looking and watching as if he was waiting for someone. He never set one foot upon the property mind you. He's just there walking down the street an' leaning on the fence post, with his eyes taking everything in. Whenever she looked his way he would avert his eyes. She could see his game and it was like a wild animal on the hunt."

Richard: "Did she know this man?"

Debbie: "She had seen him before, but she didn't know his name. She doesn't know men like that. He had a thin face. He might be one of the Portuguese or Black Irish. He had eyes like a gypsy. He frightened her. Once he passed her on the street and she smelled him. He smelled of fish."

Richard: "Could she draw this man, this stranger?"

Debbie: "Perhaps. Maybe. He had a face that a body couldn't forget, not in a lifetime."

(Richard brought in a pen and paper. Clipping it on a board, he handed it to Debbie. She sat up on the bed, her eyes still closed, and took the pen. She looked up for a long moment, then down at the blank sheet of typing paper, and she quickly made a sketch. She worked fast, and when she was done, there was a lank face drawn upon the paper. It was a face that could be seen as frightening.)

Debbie: "There, I'm not an artist, but that is like the man she saw. The man walked with a limp."

Richard: "Thank you, thank Bridget I should say. This was the man you saw that day?"

Debbie: "Yes, why do you keep pestering her?"

Richard: "How many times did she see this man?"

Debbie: "Three, maybe four times. The last time was on the day of the awful murder at the house."

Richard: "What happened that day? Could Bridget tell us about that day?"

Debbie: "She is leaving now, she has work to do."

Richard: "Can you go to her?"

Debbie: "She is gone now. All I can see is the pear tree and the barn. Things are getting dim now."

Richard: "Can you move into the house please?"

Debbie: "I am on the porch now. The door is locked."

Richard: "Can you look into the barn now? Is there anyone in the barn right now?"

Debbie: "It is fading fast. I can't keep it in focus. Let me try to…"

Richard: "Don't lose it now, we are so close."

Debbie: "Be quiet! Let me try to… Don't say anything."

(Debbie rolled onto her back, her face twisted into an expression of deep concentration tinged with panic.)

Debbie: "It's gone… The images have faded into the dark."

Richard: "Could you please try again?"

Debbie: "NO. Not tonight… I can't do it tonight. Maybe in a day or so."

The first attempt seemed to have communicated with the maid, Bridget, who, according to her testimony, was washing windows during the first murder, that of Abby Borden. The fact that she was outside eating pears might explain why she didn't hear the fatal deathblows on that hot day. The stranger that was sighted was a possible suspect as well. Oddly enough, she had seen this man before, and perhaps her fear of him was not ungrounded.

The first session had ended so abruptly that I was fearful that future attempts would fail to gain any new information. I thought at first that only a visit to the site of the murders would enable Debbie to detect more, but I soon discovered that that wouldn't be necessary.

# SESSION NUMBER TWO

After four days had passed, another session was planned. By this time, a number of black and white photographs depicting the scene of the murders in the house, as well as some of the exterior of the house and Miss Lizzie Borden herself, had been found in Agnes DeMille's book, *Lizzie Borden: A Dance of Death*. After studying the images, Debbie held the nail used in the first session. She relaxed and began to take long, measured breaths. In time, she opened her eyes.

"It's not the same," she commented, "I'm going to try to go deeper into a trance." She rested as I put on a tape of soft music, hoping that it would help her to relax.

## SHOCKING PSYCHIC SOLUTION:

The trance she spoke of isn't the sort one would see in a bad movie's interpretation of a séance, nor is it anything like the sort of trance invoked by magicians who are about to make their shapely assistants vanish, but rather it is more like a self-induced hypnotic state which clears the mind and heightens psychic ability. In this case, I was hoping that it would enable Debbie to look back in time to a place three thousand miles away in order to solve a baffling murder case.

Fifteen minutes later, I noticed the unfixed gaze in her open eyes, and I began to record my questions and responses.

Richard: "What do you see?"

Debbie: "White, the walls are white."

Richard: "Are you in a house?"

Debbie: "Yes, there is a woman in a blue dress. It is a dark blue dress, a full dress that covers much of her body."

Richard: "Is it Lizzie?"

Debbie: "No, she isn't here in this place, not now."

Richard: "Is it Abby Borden?"

Debbie: "No, it isn't Abby. She isn't doing anything; she is just sitting. She has a small book in her hand."

Richard: "Is it Bridget, the house servant?"

Debbie: "No, it isn't Bridget. She is waiting. She is waiting for him."

Richard: "She is waiting for Mr. Borden to come home?"

Debbie: "No, she is waiting for Sean. He will be waiting for her, and she must leave at that time and no other."

# The Lizzie Borden Case

Richard: "Who is Sean?  Is this Lizzie after all?"

Debbie: "No, it is Emma.  She is nervous and waiting."

Richard: "Is Sean her lover?"

Debbie: "No, he is her confederate.  She needs him."

Richard: "Is Lizzie there?"

Debbie: "She let Emma into the house.  She is below; she is talking to someone now.  Emma can hear them.  She doesn't know what to do."

Richard: "Isn't Emma in Fairhaven on the day of the murders?  Is this another time?"

Debbie: "No, it is to be today or none at all."

Richard: "Emma is in the house on that day?  This can't be right.  She was miles away at the time of the murders."

Debbie: "That is what they want you to think."

Richard: "Is she there to see her father?"

Debbie: "No, he isn't to be home.  He is never at home at this hour.  Why today?  Why is he home?"

Richard: "Where is Abby?"

Debbie: "In the bedroom."

Richard: "Is Sean coming into the house?"

Debbie: "No, he is to wait at the barn.  He is to be across the street today.  Why will he not come?"

Richard: "Can you move downstairs and see what is happening?"

## SHOCKING PSYCHIC SOLUTION:

Debbie: "There is something she must do."

Richard: "Who?"

Debbie: "Emma. She has something in a bag, a blue cloth bag."

Richard: "Could you try to go where Lizzie is located?"

Debbie: "She can hear them talking now, in the parlor."

Richard: "Who? Lizzie and Bridget?"

Debbie: "It is their father, their father. He is home now."

Richard: "I would like you to move down the stairs and into the parlor so you can see what is happening."

Debbie: "There is something that must be done."

Richard: "When I count to three you will be out of the room and in the downstairs of the house."

Debbie: "She has something… (Unintelligible speech) I… saw the paper."

Richard: "One, two, three. Where are you now?"

Debbie: "It's dark now. Dark, but it's still hot."

Richard: "Are you downstairs?"

Debbie: "It's fading! I'm losing the images."

Richard: "Try to stay with it. You are in the house…"

Debbie: "It's gone."

Richard: "Try to stay… Go back into the bedroom."

Debbie: "Sorry, I've lost it now."

We tried to refocus an hour later, but Debbie was unable to make contact. From this brief session, the concept of a man in the picture, specifically someone named Sean, was once again established. The name sounds Irish. Many of the poorer Irish had good reason to hate Mr. Borden, perhaps providing a much-needed motive for the crime.

The idea that Emma Borden wasn't at Fairhaven fifteen miles away also adds a new dimension to the story. Could she have had a hand in the crime? How was she able to secure a firm alibi? The reference to a set time, and the fact that Mr. Borden was home early, might also hint at some plan in the murders. We would wait a week before making a third attempt.

# SHOCKING PSYCHIC SOLUTION:

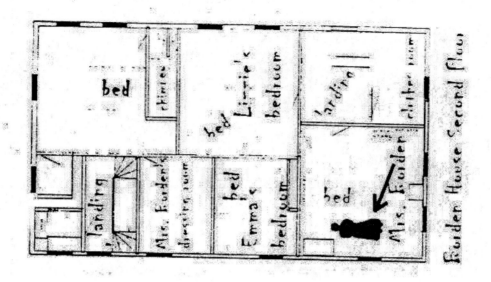

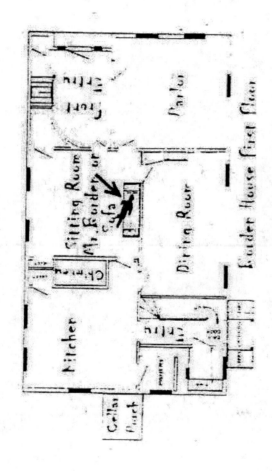

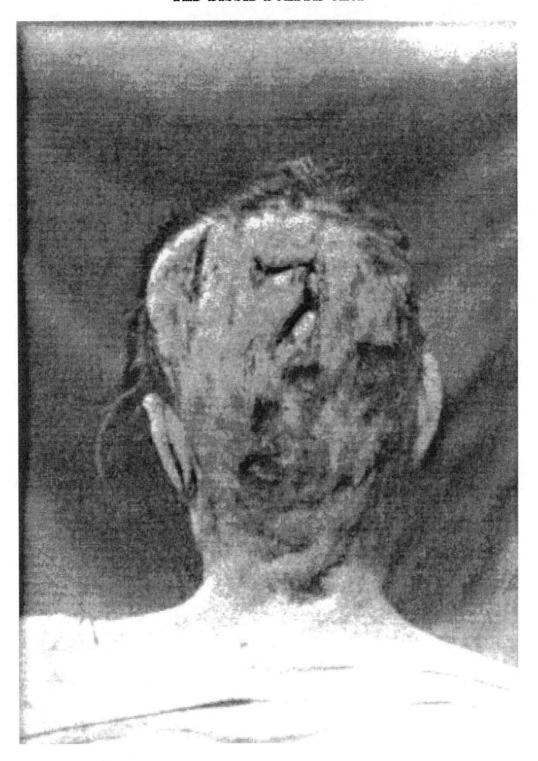

# SHOCKING PSYCHIC SOLUTION:

Emma

# SESSION NUMBER THREE

A week had passed since the last attempt and in this time a new postcard of the house was located. A floor plan of the house was given to Debbie that marked the position of the bodies. The map also listed who slept in what room. It was hoped this would help her in the next session. From what we discovered it was proving far more difficult than first imagined. Once again the nail was used and the grim pictures placed out and studied. As the clock struck nine, we started. Debbie leaned back on the pillows and began to relax. As she did I reviewed the case in my mind.  No wonder so many have pondered the case over the years.  In ten minutes I saw Debbie was in a deep trancelike state. I turned on the tape recorder and started to ask questions and take notes.

Richard: "What do you see?"

Debbie: "There is a room with a table. There are things on the table, pretty things."

Richard: "Is this upstairs or downstairs?"

Debbie: "Downstairs. There are two people talking together in a whisper. They are Lizzie and Emma. They are talking in a low voice. Emma is speaking the most. She looks so old and there is great anger in her face."

Richard: "Can you hear what they are saying?"

Debbie: "I will try. They are speaking so that no one can hear them. They are in agreement. Lizzie is shaking her head and nodding her head."

Richard: "Is this the day of the murders?"

Debbie: "No, it is before, a day or two before. I can't tell. Maybe a week?"

Richard: "Where are Abby and Andrew Borden?"

Debbie: "Eating dinner I think. They are in another room; that's why they must keep their voices so low. They do not want anyone to hear them.  Maggie? They don't want Maggie to hear."

Richard: "They called Bridget, the Irish servant girl, Maggie from time to time. Where is Maggie or Bridget?"

Debbie: "In the kitchen now, but she moves all over. They must get her out of the house.

Richard: "What are they saying?"

Debbie: "It has to be done. Emma tells Lizzie that they must act now or forever hold their peace. Abby will have everything if things continue. They will have nothing, not even mama's jewels. There is the house, she will have the property and they will be left out in the street or forced to take the scraps from HER table."

Richard: "Are they talking about Abby?"

Debbie: "Yes, their uncle overheard something that tells them that the new will leaves all to Abby. All that should be theirs will become hers. Even the things that belong rightfully to them will go to her, things that were owned by their mother."

Richard: "Are they planning to murder Abby?"

Debbie: "Poison. Rat Poison in her food."

Richard: "Is Lizzie taking part in these plans?"

Debbie: "Yes, she is the one who suggested the poison."

Richard: "So they plan to kill them both to secure the family fortune."

Debbie: "No. They only wish to slay Abby."

Richard: "Can you hear more?"

Debbie: "They are leaving. They will tell everyone about letters and threats. People will believe this. There have been threats in the past and robberies in the neighborhood and worse. People do not like Andrew in town. He has enemies. Lizzie knows a man, a hard man who hates their father—his name is Sean."

Richard: "So Sean is Lizzie's friend? Are they lovers?"

Debbie: "No. She helped him and his family once. He will help them now. They must trust him, besides who would believe a 'Mick' in town? He will help. He has a carriage he can use."

Richard: "Can you go forward in time to the day of the murders? I will count to three and when I am done counting you will be in the house August the 2nd, 1892. One, two, three. Now what do you see?"

Debbie: (pause) "They didn't sell her the poison. People suspect, maybe Abby suspects something."

Richard: "So they decided to use an axe from the kitchen?"

Debbie: "No, not an axe. Something else. Something from the farm. (Pause) Something old and silent. An Indian tomahawk, with a long handle. From the old days, the Indian times."

Richard: "Why a tomahawk?"

Debbie: "It is quiet and can kill with one blow. Everyone knows about King Philip's War (one of the early Indian Wars.) You can carry it in your skirt. No one would suspect.  It is the weapon of a savage."

Richard: "Did they hire Sean to kill Abby and Andrew?"

Debbie: "No. He only drove the carriage. He picked up Emma and drove her with a matched pair to Fall River. She walked the three blocks to the house that morning. Lizzie let her in and she went to her room."

Richard: "Where are you now?"

Debbie: "The guest bedroom. Abby is making the bed. She is on her knees. She hears someone."

Richard: "Emma?"

Debbie: "No, it's Abby. She is in the guestroom when Emma walks in. She holds the weapon behind her. Abby looks up and there is a sneer on her face. She says something sharp. Then she looks up again. The iron tomahawk comes down onto her forehead. Abby falls. The blood flies in an arc as the tomahawk comes up and down, up and down. Emma has to move in close to continue her attack. It is over in seconds. Emma turns and leaves the room."

Richard: "Did Abby scream?"

Debbie: "Oh, there was only a gasp when the first blow hit and a sound like a crunch. The she fell onto the floor."

Richard: "Did Emma check to see if she was really dead?"

Debbie: "There was no need."

Richard: "What did she do then?"

Debbie: "She closed the door and went to Lizzie's bedroom. She sat down and began reading from a little book."

Richard: "What about the tomahawk? Wasn't it dripping blood?"

Debbie: "No, she placed that into a bag, a dark blue cloth bag, a navy bag."

Richard: "Can you continue in time on the morning of the day of the murders? Can you travel forward in time?"

Debbie: "I will try…I can try…"

## SHOCKING PSYCHIC SOLUTION:

Richard: "I will count to three and you will be in the house, it is the morning of August 2nd, 1892. One, (pause) Two, (pause) Three. What do you see?"

Debbie: "Lizzie, she is at the window. She is looking out in the dim light of the dawn. There is like a mist. She is waiting for Emma. There is a tap. Lizzie opens the spring lock. She lets her sister into the house. They do not speak. Emma has soft shoes and walks upstairs. She has the bag she brought with her from Fairhaven. A long handle projects from the bag."

Richard: "Is it the murder weapon? How long is the handle?"

Debbie: "Maybe three feet. She goes to her room—or is it Lizzie's room? I can't tell."

Richard: "Where is Bridget?"

Debbie: "She isn't up yet. If she is, she is in the kitchen."

Richard: "Is anyone up?"

Debbie: "Uncle is up, even father isn't up yet. The cock has just crowed. It is just light out."

Richard: "Now I want you to travel forward in time to the period just after breakfast. When I count to three you will be at that time. One, two, three,"

Debbie: "I can't... I see something... it's Andrew I think with his vest...No, it's gone now."

Richard: "Try again, focus on Andrew."

Debbie: "Its all dark now; there are only shadows and (could not interpret tape).... Lizzie's face in a mirror. Blue dress? There is a blue dress.... No, it's fading...."

Richard: "Keep focused, what is there about a blue dress?"

# THE LIZZIE BORDEN CASE

Debbie: "It's gone now."

The sessions came to an end once again with only a few clues as to the nature of the case. Something would be needed to bring the site into her mind's eye. As a psychometrist, she needed something to touch, to hold. For a time we thought of postponing the experiment until we could travel to Fall River and tour the site of the murders. It was a very busy period for us, and we quickly became involved in a number of other projects, from filming a TV documentary on the haunted Whaley House in San Diego for the A&E Network to working on an investigation of a yacht rumored to have belonged to the gangster Al Capone. The Lizzie Borden tapes that were recorded over several nights, a project that had begun with so much promise, were left on the shelf in our study, left to gather dust.

As it would happen, events would take an interesting turn in the next four months, as the needed artifacts would come into our hands.

# Shocking Psychic Solution:

# SESSION NUMBER FOUR

Our friend Wendy R. had just visited the Fall River home of the Borden family and had learned that the owners of the house were remodeling the basement and, in doing so, they were searching for any evidence that may have been overlooked in the investigation conducted over a century ago. Specifically, they were looking for the missing axe that had been used as the murder weapon. However, they were disappointed in their search, having recovered nothing more than dirt.

Wendy asked for and received a bag of earth and a stone they found in the basement area of the house. Wendy, knowing Debbie's interest in the Lizzie Borden Case, presented the earth and stone to her when she returned to the west coast. It was an unexpected gift and one that provided a new link to the murder site. We resolved to continue the psychic quest to see what could be deduced using these new samples.  Another experiment was set up in the next few days.

I asked if Debbie wished to review the former tapes to better understand what had come from past sessions. She refused to look over past findings out of fear it might confuse her. Psychic impressions are random by their very nature. They exist in their own fluid moment and as such they defy logic and reason. In such investigations logic can hamper progress at this stage. A time would come when the data would be sifted, but that was in the future. Most reputable psychics agree with Debbie that foreknowledge can hurt attempts to gather psychic traces.

We gathered our artifacts as Debbie meditated once again. She had some of the soft earth in her hand and the stone next to her. It was 9:40 in the evening as she relaxed in bed.  I put on the relaxing music and waited ten minutes.  She was in a deep trance and ready to begin the session. I turned on the recorder and began to ask questions.

Richard: "What do you see?"

Debbie: "Darkness."

Richard: "Where are you now?"

Debbie: "Darkness is all around me."

Richard: "Are you in the basement? In a dark room?"

Debbie: "No, no. I'm in Lizzie's bedroom. She is there looking at a mirror. There is blood."

Richard: "Blood in her room?"

Debbie: "No, blood on the sofa. She keeps saying that it can't have happened. Something was wrong, very wrong. Andrew isn't the one. It was Abby. Abby was the one to be put aside not father! Something had happened. He came home at the wrong time. He wasn't to be there. The door was to have been left open. He was to come home and find the door open! That was the way it was to be. He should be alive now! With that woman gone he could give them what was theirs, his love and his wealth."

Richard: "Andrew, their father is dead now?"

Debbie: "Yes, he should not have been home."

Richard: "Who killed him? Sean?"

Debbie: "No, dear God, she loved him and he, in his way loved her. No, she couldn't hurt him even if she desired to, and she did not."

Richard: "Who Killed Andrew?"

Debbie: "Emma. Emma killed him the same way she killed Abby."

Richard: "How? Why?"

Debbie: "She used the tomahawk. She was seen by Andrew as she tried to walk down the stairs. He was on the sofa and saw her, calling out her name. She didn't know he was in the house. He thought that she was still in Fairhaven like everyone else. Once the murder was discovered he would have realized at once what the truth was and they (Lizzie and Emma) would be lost. She told him a story about being ill and he was convinced that nothing was out of the ordinary. He didn't see the bloody bag. He didn't see the long handle or if he did, he didn't say a word about it. In panic, in fear, she waited until he placed his head back and closed his eyes. She took the weapon and struck. There were tears in her eyes when she killed him. She couldn't wait any longer so she struck again and again. She ran out of the door letting it lock closed behind her."

## SHOCKING PSYCHIC SOLUTION:

Richard: "Was Lizzie in the room when this was happening?"

Debbie: "No, she was upstairs. When she came down she saw the crime and was terror filled. She began to scream almost at once."

Richard: "What of Emma?"

Debbie: "Lizzie didn't know what had happened. Perhaps another had killed Andrew? She didn't know that her father had seen Emma coming down the stairs and that he had said something. She didn't know that. How could she have known?"

Richard: "Where is Emma at this time? Could you travel to where Emma is now?"

Debbie: "Yes, I think I can. (Pause). She is in a coach or shay. Sean is driving the animals hard. They are making their way to Fairhaven. She is bouncing around in the back. She still has the bloody tomahawk in the bag. The bag is wet with blood and gore. The road is dusty and rutted. It is not a well traveled road."

Richard: "What is the name of the road?"

Debbie: "The old Post Road, I think. It's the old road."

Richard: "Will anyone see them?"

Debbie: "They will think it's another. They will go near the farm, but not too near. Emma will walk back. With luck no one will see her now."

Richard: "What about the tomahawk? What does she do with the thing?"

Debbie: "There is a dry well on the grounds of the place near the house; she will drop it into the dry well. That and the bag and the rags she used to clean away the blood from her fingers and wrist. No one will think to check or even look. Tomahawks are common here, left over from the Indian Wars."

Richard: "Why did she do it? Kill her own father?"

Debbie: "She didn't love him as Lizzie did. He never saw her in the same light as he did Lizzie. It was something she had to do to save herself. She didn't even try to think of another way out. There was only one way—blood."

Richard: "What of Sean? Could they trust him? Would he keep quiet about the crime?"

Debbie: "Sure. He would face the gallows too. He hated Andrew from a past misdeed and he owed Lizzie. He returned to the old county a rich man. He purchased a farm then, in his older years, ran a pub. He had seven children and only on his deathbed did he say a word of his past deeds to his priest and youngest daughter. They told not a soul and his involvement went with them to their graves."

Richard: "Is there any way of finding out if this Sean ever was a party to this?"

Debbie: "Yes, in Durry, he is buried now and they tell a story of this pub-man and the murders in America. The wild ride by night. Find the legend and the song and it will tell the story."

Richard: "What of the people in Fairhaven? How could Emma be so sure that she would not be suspected?"

Debbie: "Emma was sure. Money has a way of making things that are untrue fact. Few even suspected her and none could imagine the wild ride she took and the type of coach she used."

Richard: "What of Lizzie?"

Debbie: "Emma told her what had happened that night. She stood with her throughout the trial and beyond. They were united in their guilt and in the crime they had planned, the death of Abby, and the second, unplanned murder of Andrew."

Richard: "Can you travel back to where Lizzie is now?"

Debbie: "She didn't do the crime. She planned it but to her it was like a fantasy that she never had in her heart thought would happen. She did grow to hate Abby, her stepmother, but she never hated her father. It was Emma who urged her on and kept the pot boiling. The death of Andrew almost unhinged Lizzie. It was so final, so unexpected, after all the weeks and months of planning. He wasn't the planned victim. He was to find the body and the unlocked door and other clues to blame the Portuguese people in town. Things went terribly wrong."

Richard: "What other clues?"

Debbie: "It's fading now. It's going…"

Richard: "Go back to Lizzie's Room. When I count to three you will be in Lizzie's Room. One, two, three."

Debbie: "It's gone…there is no more, only darkness and sadness."

We ended the session with a discussion. I asked if she thought the Fall River area might be haunted by the ghosts of the tragedy so long ago. She took her time to formulate an answer, and then nodded her head.

# THE LIZZIE BORDEN CASE

"Yes, there is an element of unfinished work, forgiveness and pain. I think there is a ghost, maybe four, perhaps even five. Andrew, Abby, Emma, Lizzie and Bridget may well haunt the place in some form. I also think there may well be another. It is a woman who knew more than she let on at the trial."

Debbie also came away with the impression that Bridget, the Irish maid, had some bit of information that was never brought to light. This fact and others hinted at might prove what really happened that day. Many facts were kept from the public with money.

In the next two weeks Debbie and I reviewed the notes of the four sessions and the known testimony on the case. We attempted to put together a timeline of events to fit the new information gathered in our psychic detective hunt. These details show the progression of events. Next we placed in a concise form the psychic solution to the case, as we see it. We believe Debbie's skills had at long last solved the Fall River mystery.

## SHOCKING PSYCHIC SOLUTION:

# PSYCHIC SOLUTION:
# THE LIZZIE BORDEN CASE.

A psychic timeline of the murders.
(*All psychic data in italics*)

The Psychic timeline as developed by Richard and Debbie Senate. The times represented are approximations of events before and during the day of the killings.

## Shocking Psychic Solution:

July 11, 1892—Emma & Lizzie learn of changes to the will.

July 17, 1892—*Emma & Lizzie plan to poison Abby.*

July 18, 1892—Lizzie's attempt to purchase poison fails.

July 21, 1892—*Emma suggests the use of an Indian tomahawk as a means to kill Abby. The use of a 'savage' weapon will throw the blame on foreigners in town.*

July 22, 1892—*The plan is worked out. Emma will plan a trip to Fairhaven, return and kill Abby, they will use a coach from a man Lizzie befriended. The door will be left open and the story of a robbery told.*

July 26, 1892—*Details of the plan are formed.*

July 28, 1892—Lizzie and Emma leave the house. Lizzie returns and Emma goes to the Brownell house in Fairhaven.

August 2, 1892—Abby fears she has been poisoned and goes to the doctor.

August 3, 1892—Lizzie speaks to a friend about robberies and threats.

August 4, 1892—

> 4:30 a.m. *Emma leaves Fairhaven in coach.*
>
> 6:20 a.m. *Lizzie lets Emma into the house.*
>
> 7:20 a.m. Breakfast. Lizzie refuses to eat with Abby.
>
> 8:20 a.m.  Lizzie tries to get Bridget out of house.
>
> 9:00 a.m. Andrew leaves the house. Not expected back until noon.

# The Lizzie Borden Case

9:20 a.m.  *Emma surprises Abby in guest room and kills her.*

10:20 a.m.  *Coachman is late to pick up Emma.*

10:40 a.m.  Andrew comes home early due to feeling sick. Lizzie tells him Abby is out visiting a sick friend.

10:50 a.m.  *Emma tries to sneak out and is seen by Andrew.*

11:10 a.m. Emma *uses the tomahawk on sleeping father and leaves.*

11:15 a.m. *Emma takes carriage back to Fairhaven.*

11:30 a.m. Lizzie discovers body of father and screams. Doctor is called in. Lizzie is confused and upset.

12:00 *Noon* Abby's body is found in Guest Bedroom.

1:46 a.m. *Emma returns to Fairhaven.*

# Shocking Psychic Solution:

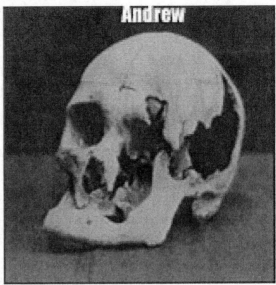

# A Conversation on the Case with
# Debbie Christenson Senate

**W**e gathered at the dining room table, the dishes and silverware were placed in the dishwasher. Only the goblets of wine rested on the white linen. The girls were listening to the Nickelodeon Channel, the sounds of cartoons echoed from the living room. We were alone and for us, like many couples with children, this was our time to discuss the happenings of the day and relate to one another as human beings and not just parents. It was then that the subject of Lizzie Borden came up.  It had come up before but this time, with the project seemingly complete, we could relax and sip the deep red wine and digest the pasta and chicken breast we had just consumed. I took out the tape recorder and turned it on to catch any stray comment or quote for the book.

"Lizzie didn't have it in her to commit a crime like that," began Debbie. "She wasn't a real doer, she could talk a good fight but she was the sort who couldn't have done anything like the murders…"

"What about the witnesses who said she had once taken a stray cat by the tail and tossed it?" I asked.

"I don't believe it for an instant," said Debbie. "Did you see how much she gave away to animal groups when she died? She loved animals. No, I think that a lot of the things that people said about her were just so much after-the- fact gossip. She was shunned by the community."

"I read that when she returned to church after the murders everyone got up from their pews and left," I added. "She was quite literally shunned."

"And she never returned to church again," confirmed Debbie. "I feel that Lizzie felt guilty over what had happened."

"Why would she feel guilty?" I inquired, pouring another glass of wine. "She didn't kill anyone, at least that we have determined in this whole investigation."

"In her mind she was as guilty as Emma. We don't know that the very notion of killing Abby may have come from Lizzie herself. Remember the poison she tried to purchase unsuccessfully just days before the crime? She may not have wielded the tomahawk but she planned the thing out and was an equal co-conspirator in the murders. She may have even felt guilty over the death of her father."

"That was unplanned, right?"

"Very much so. It wasn't needed. He was seventy years old and with Abby out of the way he would shower his attentions and money once again upon them. In the end they would have gotten it all in any case. There was no need for his death."

"So that might explain why Lizzie was so shaken when she came down to unlock the three locks on the front door, after Emma left, only to find her father hacked to death."

"Yes," smiled Debbie. "If you look at the case it is clear that some of it appears to have been well thought out and set up. The early part of the day seems to go as planned; the groundwork was set. All that was needed was for the front door to be left open and Lizzie to have some sort of alibi. Maybe she was to really go to the barn, leave footprints in the dust, and take some lead or something to put in her pockets. Things were going well when everything was upset."

"What happened?" I asked sipping the wine. "What was the one point when their well thought out plans began to unravel?"

"It was the summer sickness," explained Debbie. "The hot weather had caused the food to spoil and it made everyone sick. This even affected Andrew but, being the sort of man he was, he tried to soldier on and went in to work. But he couldn't do it and he came home early. He was a man of habit. The kind of person you could set your watch by. But this day his schedule was dramatically changed and he came home early. I believe there was some other element in the mishap as well. There may have been a misunderstanding between Emma and her driver Sean, or whatever his name was. He was seen waiting on the street by several people."

"I remember one of the books with testimony saying that such a man was seen," I added. "Wasn't there something about a black carriage too?"

## SHOCKING PSYCHIC SOLUTION:

"Yes, the stableman across the street described a strange black coach in front of the Borden House just about the time of the murder of Andrew. He noticed that the horse was a fine animal with the lines of a thoroughbred. As horses were his profession such an animal would have caught his eye. He was sure that he hadn't seen it before."

"What is a thoroughbred horse good for?" I asked knowing the answer. "Speed?"

"Yes, like a race horse," continued Debbie. "All the faster to carry Miss Emma Borden, now a rich woman, back to Fairhaven."

"But," I said, pouring another glass of wine, "the most damning evidence in the trial was given by Emma. She is the one who spoke of Lizzie burning the dress in the stove. This looked like she was throwing guilt on to her sister."

"True, but Emma didn't bring it up first, it was the other lady. I believe that Lizzie did burn a dress, or some other piece of cloth, something with blood on it. Maybe something that Emma had dripped Abby's blood on while she was waiting in Lizzie's room. Remember, Emma also was adamant on the fact that the dress was damaged by paint. I believe that Emma had another reason for this."

"What could that have been?" I wondered out loud. "Was it to frighten Lizzie into co-operation?"

"I think there was some of that in this move," speculated Debbie. "Lizzie had not planned to kill Andrew. This was a total surprise to her and one that upset the apple cart. From the point of her discovery of her father's body the case takes on a new color. Lizzie becomes confused; she starts to say things that do not make sense to anyone. The story of the trip to the barn almost becomes her undoing. The dust had not been disturbed and there was no sign of anyone coming or going. She had not had time to set up her alibi as was planned before. The evidence of the note is also interesting."

"You mean the note that she told Andrew about that Abby had received?" I said. "The one that said she should come to the assistance of a sick friend?"

"Exactly!" explained Debbie. "Abby had no friends. She never went to church; she lived at home with just the barest of contact with her neighbors. The fact that Andrew swallowed a whopper of that size is beyond comprehension. He must have been very ill to have not smelled a rat the size of a whale. The fact that Bridget overheard this and told it to the authorities must have sent a chill down Lizzie and Emma's back."

"They did offer a reward for the note, didn't they?"

"No, it was the newspaper that offered the reward I think, but no one came forth to claim it. Later, with so much scrutiny on the missing note, Lizzie made a statement that she might have accidentally burned the note in the stove. The old stove was proving useful to them. I think Lizzie was upset and confused over the way things were going and that's why Emma gave testimony about the burned dress. It pulled in the leash on Lizzie and showed her who was boss. They had to hang together or they would literally hang side by side."

"It also diverted suspicion from Emma and towards Lizzie." I observed. "Not that it was needed; everyone seemed to think Lizzie was the murderess."

"Very true."

"There never was a note?" I asked.

"No, of course not. That was a haphazard bit of quick thinking on Lizzie's part. It has all the earmarks of a bumbling attempt to keep her father from looking for Abby. It wouldn't do for him to search the upstairs and find Abby's bloody body and Emma hiding out with a blood soaked weapon. I feel that Andrew was so sick that he really wasn't that interested in where Abby was or what had been going on in his house."

"The fact that he was on the sofa must have played a part in the last act of this strange drama," I added. "From that position he could see, or at least hear, someone coming down the stairs."

"And that's how he saw Emma. I feel that he must have called out to her softly or something to make her realize that she had been recognized. When she went into the room his fate was sealed. She didn't care for Andrew the way Lizzie did and I don't think he held her in high esteem as well."

"I don't think anyone thought much about Emma," I interjected, "Over and over people called her cold and stiff. She seems a lackluster person without a shadow."

"People seemed to like Lizzie but they didn't care for Emma. This must be taken into account. If Emma had been in the dock rather than Lizzie would she have gotten off? I don't think so. Lizzie was a Sunday school teacher, a church worker; I guess that would be like a social worker today. She was still of an age when she might have married. Emma was a confirmed old maid without a real place in the community. She could well have been found guilty and suffered death on the gallows or whatever way they executed people back then. I think they were toying with the electric chair at the time."

"They were keeping up with the newest trends," I added.

"Well, whatever. The two of them were chained together by links of guilt. They would both suffer the pains of their actions for the rest of their lives."

# The Lizzie Borden Case

"I read that Lizzie, or was it Emma, was gay. Do you think that might have had something to do with the two murders?"

"I believe that there is real evidence that Lizzie was gay and she had a relationship at one point with an actress. But, what ever she did came under close public scrutiny. I think that she stayed in the closet most of her life. The years that followed the acquittal showed how much the two very different women were forced by their common guilt to stand together. At last they did part ways as their differences grew too great. In the public mind Lizzie was guilty and Emma the loyal, loving sister who was treated so poorly. I believe this was a well-cultivated lie."

"Do you think any scraps of evidence might be unearthed someday to prove this theory that Emma killed Abby and Andrew?"

"I don't know. Maybe if someone searched Fairhaven, near the place where Emma was staying, searched the wells and outhouses, places like that. Maybe they just might find an old Indian tomahawk. Maybe there is something, information, in Ireland. It might be a legend or story of the murder. Maybe the story has been twisted. New clues will not come from the Fall River or from the house; those places have been searched and searched over and over again. The mystery will continue to haunt those who are interested in the case. All I can say is that I believe that these psychic impressions solve the case. I believe that they plotted the murder of the stepmother, carried it off, then by chance, Emma, on her own, killed her father. Lizzie took the blame and stood trial. Only by the skills of her lawyers and the narrow Victorian thinking of the day did she get off. I believe Emma was haunted by the murders and lived with that guilt all the years of her life. She lived the life of a recluse until her death, unlike Lizzie, who attempted to live a life of social existence in the face of public opinion."

# Shocking Psychic Solution:

# A PSYCHIC EXPERIMENT YOU CAN TRY

Did Lizzie Borden really plot the murder of her stepmother and father? Did she wield the bloody axe as the children's rhythm declares?

> *Lizzie Borden took an Axe*
> *And gave her mother forty whacks*
> *When she saw what she had done,*
> *She gave her father forty-one.*

What do you think? We ask the readers to try their own psychic ability and challenge them to look back in time and space to that hot stuffy house in 1892. Project your own psychic eye back and see if Debbie's impressions are right. Perhaps you may find another answer or focus on some point Debbie has missed. To conduct the experiment, just follow these steps.

1. Look at the pictures of the major players in the tragedy and the floor plan of the house.

2. Read the accounts of the trial included and the words of Lizzie herself.

3. Find a place to relax, a bed or a couch. Make sure you can find a place where you will not be disturbed for at least an hour.

4. Make your mind blank and meditate. Picture in your mind a relaxing place such as the seacoast. Then, when you are relaxed, let your mind wander to Fall River. Sometimes a

friend can be helpful just as Richard helped Debbie to travel back to 1892.

5. If possible visit Fall River and the house where the murders took place. It's now a bed and breakfast so you might be able to sleep in Lizzie's Room! This would be an ideal place for your psychic time travel.

6. Try to answer these questions:

    a. Who did the crime?

    b. Why were Abby & Andrew killed?

    c. How did the killers get into the house?

    d. Who stood to gain from the crime?

    e. What happened to the murder weapon?

    f. What about the burned dress?

    g. Where was Lizzie when Andrew was killed?

    h. Why was Lizzie found not guilty?

    i. Was there a note?

    j. What did Bridget know?

    k. What is your timeline of the death day?

If you can come up with a new idea or solution, or, if you can confirm any of Debbie's insights please feel free to contact the authors at their web site:

www.ghost-stalkers.com
or contact the Phantom Bookshop
in Ventura, California.
At phantom@phantoms.com

# APPENDIX ONE

**Lizzie's interview from the jail cell to _The New York Record_, September 20, 1892 by Mrs. McGuirk. (The reporter was an old acquaintance of Lizzie Borden).**

"I know I am innocent and I have made up my mind that, no matter what happens, I will try to bear it bravely and make the best of it." The speaker was a woman. The words came slowly, and her eyes filled with tears that did not fall before they were wiped away. The woman was Lizzie Borden, who had been accused of the murders of her father, and personally has been made to appear in the eyes of the public as a monster, lacking in respect for the law, and stolid in her demeanor to such an extent that she never showed emotion at any stage of the tragedy, inquest or trial, and, as far as the government would allow they knew, had never shown any womanly or human emotion of any sort since the public first crossed the threshold of the Borden house.

I was anxious to see if this girl, with whom I was associated several years ago in the work of the Fall River Fruit and Flower

## Shocking Psychic Solution:

Mission (a church social service club), had changed her character and become a monster since the days when she used to load up the plates of vigorous young newsboys and poor children at the annual turkey dinner provided during the holidays for them and take delight in their hearty appetites.

I sought her in the Taunton jail and found her unchanged, except that she showed traces of the great trial she has just been through. Her face was thinner, her mouth had a patient look, as if she had been schooling herself to expect and to bear any treatment, however unpleasant, and her eyes were red from the long nights of weeping. A dark shade now protects them from the glaring white light reflected from the walls of her cell.

"How do you get along here, Miss Borden?" I asked.

"To tell the truth, I am afraid it is beginning to tell on my health. This lack of fresh air and exercise is hard for me. I have always been out of doors a great deal, and that makes it harder. I cannot sleep nights now, and nothing they give me will produce sleep. If it were not for my friends, I should break down, but as long as they stand by me I can bear it. They have been, with few exceptions, true to me all through it, and I appreciate it. If they had not, I don't know how I could have gone through it all. I certainly should have broken down. Some things have been very unpleasant, but while everyone has been so kind to me I ought not to think of those. Marshal Hilliard has been very gentlemanly and kind to me in every way possible.

"The hardest thing for me to stand here is the night, when there is no light. They will not allow me to have a candle to read by, and to sit in the dark all evening is very hard; but I do not want any favors that are against the rules. Mr. Wright and his wife are very kind to me and try to make it easier to bear, but of course, they must do their duty.

# THE LIZZIE BORDEN CASE

"There is one thing which hurts me very much. They say I don't show any grief. Certainly I don't in public. I never did reveal my feelings and cannot change my nature now. They say I don't cry. They should see me when I am alone, or sometimes with my friends. It hurts me to think people say so about me. I have tried very hard to be brave and womanly though it all.... It is a little thing, I suppose, but it hurt me when they said I was not willing to have my room searched. Why, I had seen so many different men that day and questioned about everything till my head was confused and in such a whirl that I could not think. I was lying down and Dr. Bowen was just preparing some medicine for me when a man came to my room and began to question me. I knew he was a policeman because he had brass buttons on his clothes. I asked the doctor:

'Must I see all these people now? It seems as if I cannot think a moment longer, my head pains me so.'

He went out. When he returned he said I must see them, and then the policeman came back with another man, they spoke about my mother, and that was the time I said, 'She's not my mother but my stepmother.' I supposed, if it was necessary that I must talk to them just then, I must tell as near as I could what was right . . . .

"If people would only do me justice, that is all I ask, but it seems as if every word I have uttered has been distorted and such a false construction placed on it that I am bewildered. I can't understand it."

# SHOCKING PSYCHIC SOLUTION:

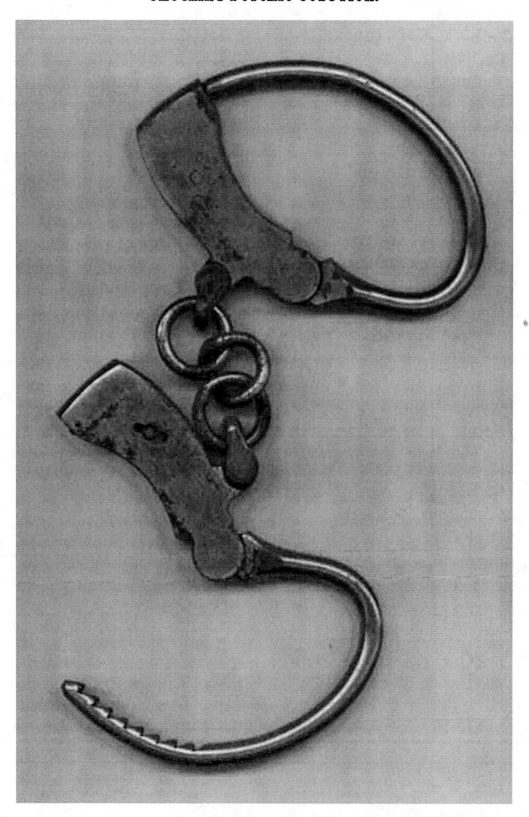

# SHOCKING PSYCHIC SOLUTION:

# APPENDIX TWO:
# THE LIZZIE BORDEN INQUEST.

## SHOCKING PSYCHIC SOLUTION:

### Questioning by District Attorney Hosea Knowlton:

Q. Give me your full name.

A. Lizzie Andrew Borden.

Q. Is it Lizzie or Elizabeth?

A. Lizzie.

Q. You were so christened?

A. I was so christened.

Q. What is your age, please?

A. Thirty-two.

Q. Your mother is not living?

A. No sir.

Q. When did she die?

A. She died when I was two-and-a-half years old.

Q. You do not remember her then?

A. No sir.

Q. What was your father's age?

A. He was 70 next month.

Q. What was his whole name?

A. Andrew Jackson Borden.

Q. And your stepmother, what is her whole name?

A. Abby Durfee Borden.

Q. How long had your father been married to your stepmother?

A. I think about 27 years.

Q. How much of that time have they lived in that house on Second Street?

A. I think, I am not sure, but I think about 20 years last May.

Q. Always occupied the whole house?

A. Yes sir.

Q. Somebody told me it was once fitted up for two tenements.

A. When we bought it it was for two tenements and the man we bought it off of stayed there a few months until he finished his own house. After he finished his own house and moved into it, there was no one else moved in. We always had the whole.

Q. Have you any idea how much your father was worth?

A. No sir.

Q. Have you ever heard him say?

A. No sir.

Q. Have you ever formed any opinion?

A. No sir.

Q. Do you know something about his real estate?

A. About what?

Q. His real estate.

A. I know what real estate he owned, part of it. I don't know whether or not I know it all or not.

Q. Tell me what you know of.

A. He owns two farms in Swansea, the place on Second Street and the A. J. Borden Building and corner and the land on South Main Street where McMannus is and then, a short time ago, he bought some real estate up further south that formerly, he said, belonged to a Mr. Birch.

Q. Did you ever deed him any property?

A. He gave us, some years ago, Grandfather Borden's house on Ferry Street and he bought that back from us some weeks ago. I don't know just how many.

Q. As near as you can recall.

A. Well, I should say in June, but I am not sure.

Q. What do you mean by 'bought it back'?

A. He bought it of us and gave us the money for it.

Q. How much was it?

A. How much money? He gave us $5,000 for it.

Q. Did you pay him anything when you took a deed from him?

A. Pay him anything? No sir.

Q. How long ago was it you took a deed from him?

A. When he gave it to us?

Q. Yes.

A. I can't tell you. I should think five years.

Q. Did you have any other business transactions with him besides that?

A. No sir.

Q. In real estate?

A. No sir.

Q. Or in personal property?

A. No sir.

Q. Never?

A. Never.

Q. No transfer of property one way or another?

A. No sir.

Q. At no time?

A. No sir.

Q. And I understand he paid you the cash for this property?

A. Yes sir.

Q. You and Emma equally?

A. Yes sir.

Q. How many children has your father?

A. Only two.

Q. Only you two?

A. Yes sir.

Q. Any others ever?

A. One that died.

Q. Did you know of your father making a will?

A. No sir, except I heard somebody say once that there was one several years ago. That is all I ever heard.

Q. Who did you hear say so?

A. I think it was Mr. Morse.

Q. What Morse?

A. Uncle John V. Morse.

Q. How long ago?

A. How long ago I heard him say it? I have not any idea.

Q. What did he say about it?

A. Nothing except just that.

Q. What?

A. That Mr. Borden had a will.

Q. Did you ask your father?

A. I did not.

Q. Did he ever mention the subject of a will to you?

A. He did not.

Q. He never told you that he had made a will or had not?

# SHOCKING PSYCHIC SOLUTION:

A. No sir.

Q. Did he have a marriage settlement with your stepmother that you know of?

A. I never knew of any.

Q. Had you heard anything of his proposing to make a will?

A. No sir.

Q. Do you know of anybody that your father was on bad terms with?

A. There was a man that came there that he had trouble with. I don't know who the man was.

Q. When?

A. I cannot locate the time exactly. It was within two weeks. That is, I don't know the date or day of the month.

Q. Tell all you saw and heard.

A. I did not see anything. I heard the bell ring and father went to the door and let him in. I did not hear anything for some time except just the voices. Then I heard the man say, "I would like to have that place; I would like to have that store." Father said, "I am not willing to let your business go in there." And the man said, "I thought with your reputation for liking money, you would let your store for anything." Father said, "You are mistaken." Then they talked a while and then their voices were louder and I heard father order him out and went to the front door with him.

Q. What did he say?

A. He said he had stayed long enough and he would thank him to go.

Q. Did he say anything about coming again?

A. No sir.

Q. Did your father say anything about coming again, or did he?

A. No sir.

Q. Have you any idea who that was?

A. No sir. I think it was a man from out of town because he said he was going home to see his partner.

Q. Have you had any efforts made to find him?

A. We have had a detective; that is all I know.

Q. You have not found him?

A. Not that I know of.

Q. You can't give us any other idea about it?

A. Nothing but what I have told you.

Q. Beside that, do you know of anybody that your father had bad feelings toward or who had bad feelings toward your father?

A. I know of one man who has not been friendly with him. They have not been friendly for years.

Q. Who?

A. Mr. Hiram C. Harrington.

Q. What relation is he to him?

A. He is my father's brother-in-law.

Q. Your mother's brother?

A. My father's only sister married Mr. Harrington.

Q. Anybody else that was on bad terms with your father or that your father was on bad terms with?

A. Not that I know of.

Q. You have no reason to suppose that the man you spoke of a week or two ago had ever seen your father before or has since?

A. No sir.

Q. Do you know of anybody that was on bad terms with your stepmother?

A. No sir.

Q. Or that your stepmother was on bad terms with?

A. No sir.

Q. Had your stepmother any property?

A. I don't know. Only that she had half the house that belonged to her father.

Q. Where was that?

A. On Fourth Street.

Q. Who lives in it?

A. Her half-sister.

Q. Any other property besides that that you know of?

A. I don't know.

Q. Did you ever know of any?

A. No sir.

Q. Did you understand that she was worth anything more than that?

A. I never knew.

Q. Did you ever have any trouble with your stepmother?

A. No sir.

Q. Have you within six months had any words with her?

A. No sir.

Q. Within a year?

A. No sir.

Q. Within two years?

A. I think not.

Q. When last that you know of?

A. About five years ago.

Q. What about?

A. Her stepsister, half-sister.

Q. What name?

A. Her name now is Mrs. George W. Whitehead.

Q. Nothing more than hard words?

A. No sir. They were not hard words. It was simply a difference of opinion.

Q. You have been on pleasant terms with your stepmother since then?

A. Yes sir.

Q. Cordial?

A. It depends upon one's idea of cordiality perhaps.

Q. According to your idea of cordiality?

A. We were friendly, very friendly.

Q. Cordial, according to your idea of cordiality?

A. Quite so.

Q. What do you mean by "quite so?"

A. Quite cordial. I do not mean the dearest of friends in the world, but very kindly feelings and pleasant. I do not know how to answer you any better than that.

Q. You did not regard her as your mother?

A. Not exactly, no, although she came there when I was very young.

Q. Were your relations toward her that of daughter and mother?

A. In some ways it was and in some it was not.

Q. In what ways was it?

A. I decline to answer.

Q. Why?

A. Because I don't know how to answer it.

Q. In what ways was it not?

A. I did not call her mother.

Q. What name did she go by?

A. Mrs. Borden.

Q. When did you begin to call her Mrs. Borden?

A. I should think five or six years ago.

Q. Before that time you had called her mother?

A. Yes sir.

Q. What led to the change?

A. The affair with her stepsister.

Q. So that the affair was serious enough to have you change from calling her mother, do you mean?

A. I did not choose to call her mother.

Q. Have you ever called her mother since?

A. Yes, occasionally.

Q. To her face, I mean?

A. Yes.

Q. Often?

A. No sir.

Q. Seldom?

A. Seldom.

Q. Your usual address was Mrs. Borden?

A. Yes sir.

Q. Did your sister Emma call her mother?

A. She always called her Abby from the time she came into the family.

Q. Is your sister Emma older than you?

A. Yes sir.

Q. What is her age?

A. She is 10 years older than I am. She was somewhere about 14 when she came there.

Q. What was your stepmother's age?

A. I don't know. I asked her sister Saturday and she said 64. I told them 67. I did not know. I told as nearly as I knew. I did not know there was so much difference between her and my father.

Q. Why did you leave off calling her mother?

A. Because I wanted to.

Q. Is that all the reason you have to give me?

A. I have not any other answer.

Q. Can't you give me any better reason than that?

A. I have not any reason to give except that I did not want to.

Q. In what respects were the relations between you and her that of mother and daughter, besides not calling her mother?

A. I don't know that any of the relations were changed. I had never been to her as a mother in many things. I always went to my sister because she was older and had the care of me after my mother died.

Q. In what respects were the relations between you and her that of mother and daughter?

A. That is the same question you asked before. I can't answer you any better now than I did before.

Q. You did not say before you could not answer, but that you declined to answer.

A. I decline to answer because I do not know what to say.

Q. That is the only reason?

A. Yes sir.

Q. You called your father, father?

A. Always.

Q. Were your father and mother happily united?

A. Why, I don't know but that they were.

Q. Why do you hesitate?

A. Because I don't know but that they were and I am telling the truth as nearly as I know it.

Q. Do you mean me to understand that they were happy entirely or not?

A. So far as I know they were.

Q. Why did you hesitate then?

A. Because I did not know how to answer you any better than what came into my mind. I was trying to think if I was telling it as I should, that's all.

Q. Do you have any difficulty in telling it as you should; any difficulty in answering my questions?

A. Some of your questions I have difficulty answering because I don't know just how you mean them.

Q. Did you ever know of any difficulty between her and your father?

A. No sir.

Q. Did he seem to be affectionate?

A. I think so.

Q. As man and woman who are married ought to be?

A. So far as I have ever had any chance of judging.

Q. They were?

A. Yes.

Q. What dress did you wear the day they were killed?

A. I had on a navy blue, sort of a Bengaline silk skirt with a navy blue blouse. In the afternoon, they thought I had better change it. I put on a pink wrapper.

Q. Did you change your clothing before the afternoon?

A. No sir.

Q. You dressed in the morning as you have described and kept that clothing on until afternoon?

A. Yes sir.

Q. When did Morse come there first? I don't mean this visit. I mean as a visitor, John V. Morse?

A. Do you mean this day that he came and stayed all night?

Q. No. Was this visit the first to your house?

A. He has been in the east a year or more.

Q. Since he has been in the east, has he been in the habit of coming to your house?

A. Yes, he came in any time he wanted to.

Q. Before that, had he been at your house---before he came east?

A. Yes, he has been here, if you remember the winter that the river was frozen over and they went across, he was here that winter, some 14 years ago, was it not?

Q. I am not answering questions but asking them.

A. I don't remember the date. He was here that winter.

Q. Has he been here since?

A. He has been here once since. I don't know whether he has or not since.

Q. How many times this last year has he been at your house?

A. None at all to speak of. Nothing more than a night or two at a time.

Q. How often did he come to spend a night or two?

A. Really, I don't know. I am away so much myself.

Q. Your last answer is that you don't know how much he had been here because you had been away yourself so much?

A. Yes.

Q. That is true the last year or since he has been east?

A. I have not been away the last year so much but other times I have been away when he has been here.

Q. Do I understand you to say that his last visit before this one was 14 years ago?

A. No. He has been here once between the two.

Q. How long did he stay then?

A. I don't know.

Q. How long ago was that?

A. I don't know.

Q. Give me your best remembrance.

A. Five or six years, perhaps six.

Q. How long has he been east this time?

A. I think over a year. I'm not sure.

Q. During the last year, how much of the time has he been at your house?

A. Very little that I know of.

Q. Your answer to that question before was, "I don't know because I have been away so much myself."

A. I did not mean I had been away very much myself in the last year.

Q. How much have you been away the last year?

A. I have been away a great deal in the daytime, occasionally at night.

Q. Where in the daytime? Any particular place?

A. No. Around town.

Q. When you go off nights, where?

A. Never, unless I have been off on a visit.

Q. When was the last time when you have been away for more than a night or two before this affair?

A. I don't think I have been away to stay more than a night or two since I came from abroad, except about three or four weeks ago I was in New Bedford for three or four days.

Q. Where at New Bedford?

A. At 20 Madison Street.

Q. How long ago were you abroad?

A. I was abroad in 1890.

Q. When did he come to the house the last time before your father and mother were killed?

A. He stayed there all night Wednesday night.

Q. My question is when he came there.

A. I don't know. I was not home when he came. I was out.

Q. When did you first see him there?

A. I did not see him at all.

Q. How did you know he was there?

A. I heard his voice.

Q. You did not see him Wednesday evening?

A. I did not. I was out Wednesday evening.

Q. You did not see him Thursday morning?

# Shocking Psychic Solution:

A. I did not. He was out when I came downstairs.

Q. When was the first time you saw him?

A. Thursday noon.

Q. You had never seen him before that?

A. No sir.

Q. Where were you Wednesday evening?

A. I spent the evening with Miss Russell.

Q. As near as you can remember, when did you return?

A. About nine o'clock at night.

Q. The family had then retired?

A. I don't know whether they had or not. I went right to my room. I don't remember.

Q. You did not look to see?

A. No sir.

Q. Which door did you come in at?

A. The front door.

Q. Did you lock it?

A. Yes sir.

Q. For the night?

A. Yes sir.

Q. And went right upstairs to your room?

A. Yes sir.

Q. When was it that you heard the voice of Mr. Morse?

A. I heard him down there about suppertime No, it was earlier than that. I heard him down there somewhere about three o'clock, I think. I was in my room Wednesday, not feeling well, all day.

Q. Did you eat supper at home Wednesday night?

A. I was at home. I did not eat any supper because I did not feel able to eat supper. I had been sick.

Q. You did not come down to supper?

A. No sir.

Q. Did you hear him eating supper?

A. No sir. I did not know whether he was there or not.

Q. You heard him in the afternoon?

A. Yes sir.

Q. Did you hear him go away?

A. I did not.

Q. You did not go down to see him?

A. No sir.

Q. Were you in bed?

A. No sir, I was on the lounge.

Q. Why did you not go down?

A. I did not care to go down and I was not feeling well and kept to my room all day.

Q. You felt better in the evening?

A. Not very much better. I thought I would go out and see if the air would make me feel any better.

Q. When you came back at nine o'clock, you did not look in to see if the family was up?

A. No sir.

Q. Why not?

A. I very rarely do when I come in.

Q. You go right to your room?

A. Yes sir.

Q. Did you have a night key?

A. Yes sir.

Q. How did you know it was right to lock the front door?

A. That was always my business.

Q. How many locks did you fasten?

A. The spring locks itself and there is a key to turn and you manipulate the bolt.

Q. You manipulated all those?

A. I used them all.

Q. Then you went to bed?

A. Yes, directly.

Q. When you got up the next morning, did you see Mr. Morse?

A. I did not.

Q. Had the family breakfasted when you came down?

A. Yes sir.

Q. What time did you come downstairs?

A. As near as I can remember, it was a few minutes before nine.

Q. Who did you find downstairs when you came down?

A. Maggie and Mrs. Borden.

Q. Did you inquire for Mr. Morse?

A. No sir.

Q. Did you suppose he had gone?

A. I did not know whether he had or not. He was not there.

Q. Your father was there?

A. Yes sir.

Q. Then you found him?

A. Yes sir.

Q. Did you speak either to your father or Mrs. Borden?

A. I spoke to them all.

Q. About Mr. Morse?

A. I did not mention him.

Q. Did not inquire anything about him?

A. No sir.

Q. How long before that time had he been at the house?

A. I don't know.

Q. As near as you can tell.

A. I don't know. He was there in June some time. I don't know whether he was there after that or not.

Q. Why did you not go to Marion with the party that went?

A. Because they went sooner than I could and I was going Monday.

Q. Why did they go sooner than you could? What was there to keep you?

A. I had taken the secretaryship and treasurer of our CE Society, had the charge, and the roll call was the first Sunday in August and I felt I must be there and attend to that part of the business.

Q. Where was your sister Emma that day?

A. What day?

Q. The day your father and Mrs. Borden were killed.

A. She had been in Fairhaven.

Q. Had you written to her?

A. Yes sir.

Q. When was the last time you wrote to her?

A. Thursday morning; and my father mailed the letter for me.

Q. Did she get it at Fairhaven?

A. No sir, it was sent back. She did not get it at Fairhaven for we telegraphed for her and she got home here Thursday afternoon and the letter was sent back to this post office.

Q. How long had she been in Fairhaven?

A. Just two weeks to the day.

Q. You did not visit in Fairhaven?

A. No sir.

Q. Had there been anybody else around the house that week, or premises?

A. No one that I know of except the man that called to see him on this business about the store.

Q. Was that that week?

A. Yes sir.

Q. I misunderstand you probably. I thought you said a week or two before.

A. No, I said that week. There was a man came the week before and gave up some keys and I took them.

Q. Do you remember of anybody else being then around the premises that week?

A. Nobody that I know of or saw.

Q. Nobody at work there?

A. No sir.

Q. Nobody doing any chores there?

A. No sir, not that I know of.

Q. Nobody had access to the house so far as you know during that time?

A. No sir.

Q. I ask you once more how it happened that, knowing Mr. Morse was at your house, you did not step in and greet him before you retired.

A. I have no reason except that I was not feeling well Wednesday and so did not come down.

Q. No, you were down when you came in from out.

A. Do you mean Wednesday night?

Q. Yes.

A. Because I hardly ever do go in. I generally went right up to my room and I did that night.

Q. Could you then get to your room from the back hall?

A. No sir.

Q. From the back stairs?

A. No sir.

Q. Why not? What would hinder?

A. Father's bedroom door was kept locked and his door into my room was locked and hooked, too, I think, and I had no keys.

Q. That was the custom of the establishment?

A. It had always been so.

Q. It was so Wednesday and so Thursday?

A. It was so Wednesday but Thursday they broke the door open.

Q. That was after the crowd came. Before the crowd came?

A. It was so.

Q. There was no access, except one had a key, and one would have to have two keys?

A. They would have to have two keys if they went up the back way to get into my room. If they were in my room, they would have to have a key to get into his room and another key to get into the back stairs.

Q. Where did Mr. Morse sleep?

A. In the next room, over the parlor in front of the stairs.

Q. Right up the stairs where your room was?

A. Yes sir.

Q. How far from your room?

A. A door opened into it.

Q. The two rooms connected directly?

A. By one door, that is all.

Q. Not through the hall?

A. No sir.

Q. Was the door locked?

A. It has been locked and bolted and a large writing desk in my room kept up against it.

Q. Then it was not a practical opening?

A. No sir.

Q. How otherwise do you get from your room to the other room?

A. I have to go into the front hall.

Q. How far apart are the two doors?

A. Very near. I don't think more than so far. (Indicating.)

Q. Was it your habit when you were in your room to keep your door shut?

A. Yes sir.

Q. That time---that Wednesday afternoon?

A. My door was open part of the time and part of the time I tried to get a nap and their voices annoyed me and I closed it. I kept it open in summer, more or less, and closed in winter.

Q. Then, unless for some special reason, you kept your door open in the summer?

A. Yes sir, if it was a warm day. If it was a cool day, I should have closed it.

Q. Where was your father when you came down Thursday morning?

A. Sitting in the sitting room in his large chair, reading the Providence Journal.

Q. Where was your mother? Do you prefer me to call her Mrs. Borden?

A. I had as soon you call her mother. She was in the dining room with a feather duster dusting.

Q. When she dusted, did she wear something over her head?

A. Sometimes when she swept, but not when dusting.

Q. Where was Maggie?

A. Just came in the back door with the long pole, brush and put the brush on the handle and getting her pail of water. She was going to wash the windows around the house. She said Mrs. Borden wanted her to.

Q. Did you get your breakfast that morning?

A. I did not eat any breakfast. I did not feel as though I wanted any.

Q. Did you get any breakfast that morning?

A. I don't know whether I ate half a banana. I don't think I did.

Q. You drank no tea or coffee that morning?

A. No sir.

Q. And ate no cookies?

A. I don't know whether I did or not. We had some molasses cookies. I don't know whether I ate any that morning or not.

Q. Were the breakfast things put away when you got down?

A. Everything except the coffee pot. I'm not sure whether that was on the stove or not.

Q. You said nothing about Mr. Morse to your father or mother?

A. No sir.

Q. What was the next thing that happened after you got down?

A. Maggie went out of doors to wash the windows and father came out into the kitchen and said he did not know whether he would go down to the post office or not. And then I sprinkled some handkerchiefs to iron.

Q. Tell us again what time you came downstairs.

A. It was a little before nine, I should say. About quarter. I don't know for sure.

Q. Did your father go downtown?

A. He went down later.

Q. What time did he start away?

A. I don't know.

Q. What were you doing when he started away?

A. I was in the dining room, I think. Yes, I had just commenced, I think, to iron.

Q. It may seem a foolish question. How much of an ironing did you have?

A. I only had about eight or ten of my best handkerchiefs.

Q. Did you let your father out?

A. No sir, he went out himself.

Q. Did you fasten the door after him?

A. No sir.

Q. Did Maggie?

A. I don't know. When she went upstairs, she always locked the door. She had charge of the back door.

Q. Did she go out after a brush before your father went away?

A. I think so.

Q. Did you say anything to Maggie?

A. I did not.

Q. Did you say anything about washing the windows?

A. No sir.

Q. Did you speak to her?

A. I think I told her I did not want any breakfast.

Q. You do not remember of talking about washing the windows?

A. I don't remember whether I did or not. I don't remember it. Yes, I remember. Yes, I asked her to shut the parlor blinds when she got through because the sun was so hot.

Q. About what time do you think your father went downtown?

A. I don't know. It must have been about nine o'clock. I don't know what time it was.

Q. You think at that time you had begun to iron your handkerchiefs?

A. Yes sir.

Q. How long a job was that?

A. I did not finish them. My flats were not hot enough.

Q. How long a job would it have been if the flats had been right?

A. If they had been hot, not more than 20 minutes, perhaps.

Q. How long did you work on the job?

A. I don't know, sir.

## SHOCKING PSYCHIC SOLUTION:

Q. How long was your father gone?

A. I don't know that.

Q. Where were you when he returned?

A. I was down in the kitchen.

Q. What doing?

A. Reading an old magazine that had been left in the cupboard, an old Harper's magazine.

Q. Had you got through ironing?

A. No sir.

Q. Had you stopped ironing?

A. Stopped for the flats.

Q. Were you waiting for them to be hot?

A. Yes sir.

Q. Was there a fire in the stove?

A. Yes sir.

Q. When your father went away, you were ironing then?

A. I had not commenced, but I was getting the little ironing board and the flannel.

Q. Are you sure you were in the kitchen when your father returned?

A. I am not sure whether I was there or in the dining room.

Q. Did you go back to your room before your father returned?

A. I think I did carry up some clean clothes.

Q. Did you stay there?

A. No sir.

Q. Did you spend any time up the front stairs before your father returned?

A. No sir.

Q. Or after he returned?

A. No sir. I did stay in my room long enough when I went up to sew a little piece of tape on a garment.

Q. Was that the time when your father came home?

A. He came home after I came downstairs.

Q. You were not upstairs when he came home?

A. I was not upstairs when he came home, no sir.

Q. What was Maggie doing when your father came home?

A. I don't know whether she was there or whether she had gone upstairs. I can't remember.

Q. Who let your father in?

A. I think he came to the front door and rang the bell and I think Maggie let him in and he said he had forgotten his key. So I think she must have been downstairs.

Q. His key would have done him no good if the locks were left as you left them?

A. But they were always unbolted in the morning.

Q. Who unbolted them that morning?

A. I don't think they had been unbolted. Maggie can tell you.

Q. If he had not forgotten his key, it would have been no good.

A. No, he had his key and could not get in. I understood Maggie to say he said he had forgotten his key.

Q. You did not hear him say anything about it?

A. I heard his voice, but I don't know what he said.

Q. I understood you to say he said he had forgotten his key.

A. No, it was Maggie said he said he had forgotten his key.

Q. Where was Maggie when the bell rang?

A. I don't know, sir.

## SHOCKING PSYCHIC SOLUTION:

Q. Where were you when the bell rang?

A. I think in my room upstairs.

Q. Then you were upstairs when your father came home?

A. I don't know sure, but I think so.

Q. What were you doing?

A. As I say, I took up these clean clothes and stopped and basted a little piece of tape on a garment.

Q. Did you come down before your father was let in?

A. I was on the stairs coming down when she let him in.

Q. Then you were upstairs when your father came to the house on his return?

A. I think I was.

Q. How long had you been there?

A. I had only been upstairs long enough to take the clothes up and baste the little loop on the sleeve. I don't think I had been up there over five minutes.

Q. Was Maggie still engaged in washing windows when your father got back?

A. I don't know.

Q. You remember, Miss Borden, I will call to your attention to it so as to see if I have any misunderstanding, not for the purpose of confusing you, you remember that you told me several times that you were downstairs and not upstairs when your father came home? You have forgotten, perhaps?

A. I don't know what I have said. I have answered so many questions and I am so confused I don't know one thing from another. I am telling you just as nearly as I know how.

Q. Calling your attention to what you said about that a few minutes ago, and now again to the circumstances, you have said you were upstairs when the bell rang and were on the stairs when Maggie let your father in, which now is your recollection of the true statement of the matter? That you were downstairs when the bell rang and your father came?

A. I think I was downstairs in the kitchen.

Q. And then you were not upstairs?

A. I think I was not because I went up almost immediately, as soon as I went down, and then came down again and stayed down.

Q. What had you in your mind when you said you were on the stairs as Maggie let your father in?

A. The other day somebody came there and she let them in and I was on the stairs. I don't know whether the morning before or when it was.

Q. You understood I was asking you exactly and explicitly about this fatal day?

A. Yes sir.

Q. I now call your attention to the fact that you had specifically told me you had gone upstairs and had been there about five minutes when the bell rang and were on your way down and were on the stairs when Maggie let your father in that day.

A. Yes, I said that. And then I said I did not know whether I was on the stairs or in the kitchen.

Q. Now how will you have it?

A. I think, as nearly as I know, I think I was in the kitchen.

Q. How long was your father gone?

A. I don't know, sir. Not very long.

Q. An hour?

A. I should not think so.

Q. Will you give me the best story you can, so far as your recollection serves you, of your time while he was gone?

## Shocking Psychic Solution:

A. I sprinkled my handkerchiefs and got my ironing board and took them in the dining room. I took the ironing board in the dining room and left the handkerchiefs in the kitchen on the table and whether I ate any cookies or not, I don't remember. Then I sat down looking at the magazine, waiting for the flats to heat. Then I went in the sitting room and got the Providence Journal and took that into the kitchen. I don't recollect of doing anything else.

Q. Which did you read first, the Journal or the magazine?

A. The magazine.

Q. You told me you were reading the magazine when your father came back.

A. I said in the kitchen, yes.

Q. Was that so?

A. Yes, I took the Journal out to read and had not read it. I had it near me.

Q. You said a minute or two ago you read the magazine a while and then went and got the Journal and took it out to read.

A. I did, but I did not read it. I tried my flats then.

Q. And went back to reading the magazine?

A. I took the magazine up again, yes.

Q. When did you last see your mother?

A. I did not see her after when I went down in the morning and she was dusting the dining room.

Q. Where did you or she go then?

A. I don't know where she went. I know where I was.

Q. Did you or she leave the dining room first?

A. I think I did. I left her in the dining room.

Q. You never saw her or heard her afterwards?

A. No sir.

Q. Did she say anything about making the bed?

A. She said she had been up and made the bed up fresh and had dusted the room and left it all in order. She was going to put some fresh pillow slips on the small pillows at the foot of the bed and was going to close the room because she was going to have company Monday and she wanted everything in order.

Q. How long would it take to put on the pillowslips?

A. About two minutes.

Q. How long to do the rest of the things?

A. She had done that when I came down.

Q. All that was left was what?

A. To put on the pillowslips.

Q. Can you give me any suggestion as to what occupied her when she was up there, when she was struck dead?

A. I don't know of anything except she had some cotton cloth pillow cases up there and she said she was going to commence to work on them. That is all I know. And the sewing machine was up there.

Q. Whereabouts was the sewing machine?

A. In the corner between the north and west side.

Q. Did you hear the sewing machine going?

A. I did not.

Q. Did you see anything to indicate that the sewing machine had been used that morning?

A. I had not. I did not go in there until after everybody had been in there and the room had been overhauled.

Q. If she had remained downstairs, you would undoubtedly have seen her?

# SHOCKING PSYCHIC SOLUTION:

A. If she had remained downstairs, I should have. If she had remained in her room, I should not have.

Q. Where was that?

A. Over the kitchen.

Q. To get to that room she would have to go through the kitchen?

A. To get up the back stairs.

Q. That is the way she was in the habit of going?

A. Yes sir, because the other doors were locked.

Q. If she had remained downstairs or had gone to her own room, you undoubtedly would have seen her?

A. I should have seen her if she had stayed downstairs. If she had gone to her room, I would not have seen her.

Q. She was found a little after 11 in the spare room. If she had gone to her own room, she must have gone through the kitchen and up the back stairs and subsequently have gone down and gone back again?

A. Yes sir.

Q. Have you any reason to suppose you would not have seen her if she had spent any portion of the time in her room or downstairs?

A. There is no reason why I should not have seen her if she had been down there, except when I first came downstairs, for two or three minutes, I went down cellar to the water closet.

Q. After that, you were where you practically commanded the view of the first story the rest of the time?

A. I think so.

Q. When you went upstairs for a short time, as you say you did, you then went in sight of the sewing machine?

A. No, I did not see the sewing machine because she had shut that room up.

Q. What do you mean?

A. I mean the door was closed. She said she wanted it kept closed to keep the dust and everything out.

Q. Was it a room with a window?

A. It has three windows.

Q. A large room?

A. The size of the parlor; a pretty fair-sized room.

Q. It is the guest room?

A. Yes, the spare room.

Q. Where the sewing machine was was the guest room?

A. Yes sir.

Q. I ask again, perhaps you have answered all you care to, what explanation can you give, can you suggest, as to what she was doing from the time she said she had got the work all done in the spare room, until 11 o'clock?

A. I suppose she went up and made her own bed.

Q. That would be in the back part?

A. Yes sir.

Q. She would have to go by you twice to do that?

A. Unless she went when I was in my room that few minutes.

Q. That would not be time enough for her to go and make her own bed and come back again.

A. Sometimes she stayed up longer and sometimes shorter. I don't know.

Q. Otherwise than that, she would have to go in your sight?

A. I should have to have seen her once. I don't know that I need to have seen her more than once.

Q. You did not see her at all?

## SHOCKING PSYCHIC SOLUTION:

A. No sir, not after the dining room.

Q. What explanation can you suggest as to the whereabouts of your mother from the time you saw her in the dining room and she said her work in the spare room was all done, until 11 o'clock?

A. I don't know. I think she went back into the spare room and whether she came back again or not, I don't know. That has always been a mystery.

Q. Can you think of anything she could be doing in the spare room?

A. Yes sir. I know what she used to do sometimes. She kept her best cape she wore on the street in there and she used occasionally to go up there to get it and to take it into her room. She kept a great deal in the guest room drawers. She used to go up there and get things and put things. She used those drawers for her own use.

Q. That connects her with her own room again, to reach which she had to go downstairs and come up again.

A. Yes.

Q. Assuming that she did not go into her own room, I understand you to say she could not have gone to her own room without your seeing her.

A. She could while I was down cellar.

Q. You went down immediately you came down, within a few minutes, and you did not see her when you came back.

A. No sir.

Q. After the time she must have remained in the guest chamber?

A. I don't know.

Q. So far as you can judge?

A. So far as I can judge she might have been out of the house or in the house.

Q. Had you any knowledge of her going out of the house?

A. She told me she had had a note. Somebody was sick and she said, "I am going to get the dinner on the way" and asked me what I wanted for dinner.

Q. Did you tell her?

A. Yes, I told her I did not want anything.

Q. Then why did you not suppose she had gone?

A. I supposed she had gone.

Q. Did you hear her come back?

A. I did not hear her go or come back, but I supposed she went.

Q. When you found your father dead, you supposed your mother had gone?

A. I did not know. I said to the people who came in, "I don't know whether Mrs. Borden is out or in. I wish you would see if she is in her room."

Q. You supposed she was out at the time?

A. I understood so. I did not suppose anything about it.

Q. Did she tell you where she was going?

A. No sir.

Q. Did she tell you who the note was from?

A. No sir.

Q. Did you ever see the note?

A. No sir.

Q. Do you know where it is now?

A. No sir.

Q. She said she was going out that morning?

A. Yes sir.

Q. I shall have to ask you once more about that morning. Do you know what the family ate for breakfast?

A. No sir.

Q. Had the breakfast all been cleared away when you got down?

A. Yes sir.

Q. I want you to tell me just where you found the people when you got down that you did find there.

A. I found Mrs. Borden in the dining room. I found my father in the sitting room.

Q. And Maggie?

A. Maggie was coming in the back door with her pail and brush.

Q. Tell me what talk you had with your mother at the time?

A. She asked me how I felt. I said I felt better than I did Tuesday, but I did not want any breakfast. She asked me what I wanted for dinner. I told her nothing. She said she was going out and would get the dinner. That is the last I saw her.

Q. Where did you go to then?

A. Into the kitchen.

Q. Where then?

A. Down cellar.

Q. Gone perhaps five minutes?

A. Perhaps not more than that. Possibly a little bit more.

Q. When you came back did you see your mother?

A. I did not. I supposed she had gone out.

Q. She did not tell you where she was going?

A. No sir.

Q. When you came back, was your father there?

A. Yes sir.

Q. What was he doing?

A. Reading the paper.

Q. Did you eat any breakfast?

A. No sir. I don't remember whether I ate a molasses cookie or not.

I did not eat any regularly prepared breakfast.

Q. Was it was usual for your mother to go out?

A. Yes sir, she went out every morning nearly and did the marketing.

Q. Was it usual for her to go away from dinner?

A. Yes sir, sometimes, not very often.

Q. How often, say?

A. Oh I should not think more than---well, I don't know, more than once in three months, perhaps.

Q. Now I call your attention to the fact that twice yesterday you told me, with some explicitness, that when your father came in, you were just coming downstairs.

A. No I did not. I beg your pardon.

Q. That you were on the stairs at the time your father was let in, you said with explicitness. Do you now say that you did not say so?

A. I said I thought first I was on the stairs; then I remembered I was in the kitchen when he came in.

Q. First you thought you were in the kitchen; afterwards, you remembered you were on the stairs?

A. As I said, I thought I was on the stairs. Then I remembered I was in the kitchen when he came in.

Q. Did you go into the front part of the house after your father came in?

A. After he came in from down the street, I was in the sitting room with him.

Q. Did you go into the front hall afterwards?

A. No sir.

Q. At no time?

A. No sir.

Q. Excepting the two or three minutes you were down cellar, were you away from the house until your father came in?

A. No sir.

Q. You were always in the kitchen or dining room, excepting when you went upstairs?

A. I went upstairs before he went out.

Q. You mean you went up there to sew a button on?

A. I basted a piece of tape on.

Q. Do you remember you did not say that yesterday?

A. I don't think you asked me. I told you yesterday I went upstairs directly after I came up from down cellar, with the clean clothes.

Q. You now say after your father went out, you did not go upstairs at all?

A. No sir, I did not.

Q. When Maggie came in there washing the windows, you did not appear from the front part of the house?

A. No sir.

Q. When your father was let in, you did not appear from upstairs?

A. No sir, I was in the kitchen.

Q. That is so?

A. Yes sir, to the best of my knowledge.

Q. After your father went out, you remained there, either in the kitchen or dining room all the time?

A. I went into the sitting room long enough to direct some paper wrappers.

Q. One of the three rooms?

A. Yes sir.

Q. So it would have been extremely difficult for anybody to have gone through the kitchen and dining room and front hall without your seeing them?

A. They could have gone from the kitchen into the sitting room while I was in the dining room, if there was anybody to go.

Q. Then into the front hall?

A. Yes sir.

Q. You were in the dining room ironing?

A. Yes sir, part of the time.

Q. You were in all the three rooms?

A. Yes sir.

Q. A large portion of that time the girl was out of doors?

A. I don't know where she was. I did not see her. I supposed she was out of doors, as she had the pail and brush.

Q. You knew she was washing windows?

A. She told me she was going to. I did not see her do it.

Q. For a large portion of the time, you did not see the girl?

A. No sir.

Q. So far as you know, you were alone in the lower part of the house a large portion of the time after your father went away and before he came back?

A. My father did not go away, I think, until somewhere about 10, as near as I can remember. He was with me downstairs.

Q. A large portion of the time after your father went away and before he came back, so far as you know, you were alone in the house?

A. Maggie had come in and gone upstairs.

Q. After he went out and before he came back, a large portion of the time after your father went out and before he came back, so far as you know, you were the only person in the house?

A. So far as I know, I was.

Q. And during that time, so far as you know, the front door was locked?

A. So far as I know.

Q. And never was unlocked at all?

A. I don't think it was.

Q. Even after your father came home, it was locked up again?

A. I don't know whether she locked it up again after that or not.

Q. It locks itself?

A. The spring lock opens.

Q. It fastens it so it cannot be opened from the outside?

A. Sometimes you can press it open.

Q. Have you any reason to suppose the spring lock was left so it could be pressed open from the outside?

A. I have no reason to suppose so.

Q. Nothing about the lock was changed before the public came?

A. Nothing that I know of.

Q. What were you doing in the kitchen when your father came home?

A. I think I was eating a pear when he came in.

Q. What had you been doing before that?

A. Been reading a magazine.

Q. Were you making preparations to iron again?

A. I had sprinkled my clothes and was waiting for the flat. I sprinkled the clothes before he went out.

Q. Had you built up the fire again?

A. I put in a stick of wood. There was a few sparks. I put in a stick of wood to try to heat the flat.

Q. You had then started the fire?

A. Yes sir.

Q. The fire was burning when he came in?

A. No sir, but it was smoldering and smoking as though it would come up.

Q. Did it come up after he came in?

A. No sir.

Q. Did you do any more ironing?

A. I did not. I went in with him and did not finish.

Q. You did not iron any more after your father came in?

A. No sir.

Q. Was the ironing board put away?

A. No sir, it was on the dining room table.

Q. When was it put away?

A. I don't know. Somebody put it away after the affair happened.

Q. You did not put it away?

A. No sir.

## SHOCKING PSYCHIC SOLUTION:

Q. Was it on the dining room table when you found your father killed?

A. I suppose so.

Q. You had not put it away then?

A. I had not touched it.

Q. How soon after your father came in before Maggie went upstairs?

A. I don't know. I did not see her.

Q. Did you see her after your father came in?

A. Not after she let him in.

Q. How long was your father in the house before you found him killed?

A. I don't know exactly because I went out to the barn. I don't know what time he came home. I don't think he had been home more than 15 or 20 minutes. I am not sure.

Q. When you went out to the barn, where did you leave your father?

A. He had laid down on the living room lounge, taken off his shoes and put on his slippers and taken off his coat and put on the reefer. I asked him if he wanted the window left that way.

Q. Where did you leave him?

A. On the sofa.

Q. Was he asleep?

A. No sir.

Q. Was he reading?

A. No sir.

Q. What was the last thing you said to him?

A. I asked him if he wanted the window left that way. Then I went into the kitchen and from there to the barn.

Q. Whereabouts in the barn did you go?

A. Upstairs.

Q. To the second story of the barn?

A. Yes sir.

Q. How long did you remain there?

A. I don't know. Fifteen or 20 minutes.

Q. What doing?

A. Trying to find lead for a sinker.

Q. What made you think there would be lead for a sinker up there?

A. Because there was some there.

Q. Was there not some by the door?

A. Some pieces of lead by the open door, but there was a box full of old things upstairs.

Q. Did you bring any sinker back from the barn?

A. Nothing but a piece of a chip I picked up on the floor.

Q. Where was that box you say was upstairs, containing lead?

A. There was a kind of a workbench.

Q. Is it there now?

A. I don't know sir.

Q. How long since you have seen it there?

A. I have not been out there since that day.

Q. Had you been in the barn before?

A. That day? No sir.

Q. How long since you had been in the barn before?

A. I don't think I had been into it, I don't know as I had, in three months.

Q. When you went out, did you unfasten the screen door?

A. I unhooked it to get out.

Q. It was hooked until you went out?

    A. Yes sir.

Q. It had been left hooked by Bridget, if she was the last one in?

    A. I suppose so. I don't know.

Q. Do you know when she did get through washing the outside?

    A. I don't know.

Q. Did you know she washed the windows inside?

    A. I don't know.

Q. Did you see her washing the windows inside?

    A. I don't know.

Q. You don't know whether she washed the dining room window and sitting room windows inside?

    A. I did not see her.

Q. If she did, would you not have seen her?

    A. I don't know. She might be in one room and I in another.

Q. Do you think she might have gone to work and washed all the windows in the dining room and you not know it?

    A. I don't know, I am sure, whether I should or not. I might have seen her and not know it.

Q. Miss Borden, I am trying in good faith to get all the doings that morning, of yourself and Miss Sullivan and I have not succeeded in doing it. Do you desire to give me any information or not?

    A. I don't know it! I don't know what your name is!

Q. It is certain beyond reasonable doubt she was engaged in washing the windows in the dining room or sitting room when your father came home. Do you mean to say you know nothing of either of those operations?

A. I knew she washed the windows outside; that is, she told me so. She did not wash the windows in the kitchen because I was in the kitchen most of the time.

Q. The dining room and sitting room, I said.

A. I don't know.

Q. It is reasonably certain she washed the windows in the dining room and sitting room inside while your father was out and was engaged in that operation when your father came home. Do you mean to say you know nothing of it?

A. I don't know whether she washed the windows in the sitting room and dining room or not.

Q. Can you give me any information how it happened at that particular time you should go into the chamber of the barn to find a sinker to go to Marion with to fish the next Monday?

A. I was going to finish my ironing. My flats were not hot. I said to myself, "I will go and try and find that sinker. Perhaps by the time I get back, the flats will be hot". That is the only reason.

Q. How long had you been reading an old magazine before you went to the barn at all?

A. Perhaps half an hour.

Q. Had you got a fish line?

A. Not here. We had some at the farm.

Q. Had you got a fishhook?

A. No sir.

Q. Had you got any apparatus for fishing at all?

A. Yes, over there.

Q. Had you any sinkers over there?

A. I think there were some. It is so long since I have been there; I think there were some.

## SHOCKING PSYCHIC SOLUTION:

Q. You had no reason to suppose you were lacking sinkers?

A. I don't think there were any on my lines.

Q. Where were your lines?

A. My fish lines were at the farm here.

Q. What made you think there were no sinkers at the farm on your lines?

A. Because some time ago when I was there, I had none.

Q. How long since you used the fish lines?

A. Five years, perhaps.

Q. You left them at the farm then?

A. Yes sir.

Q. And you have not seen them since?

A. Yes sir.

Q. It occurred to you after your father came in it would be a good time to go to the barn after sinkers and you had no reason to suppose there was not abundance of sinkers at the farm and abundance of lines?

A. The last time I was there, there were some lines.

Q. Did you not say before you presumed there were sinkers at the farm?

A. I don't think I said so.

Q. You did say so exactly. Do you now say you presume there were not sinkers at the farm?

A. I don't think there were any fishing lines suitable to use at the farm. I don't think there were any sinkers on any line that had been mine.

Q. Do you remember telling me you presumed there were lines and sinkers and hooks at the farm?

# The Lizzie Borden Case

A. I said there were lines, I thought, and perhaps hooks. I did not say I thought there were sinkers on my lines. There was another box of lines over there beside mine.

Q. You thought there were not sinkers?

A. Not on my lines.

Q. Not sinkers at the farm?

A. I don't think there were any sinkers at the farm. I don't know whether there were or not.

Q. Did you then think there were no sinkers at the farm?

A. I thought there were no sinkers anywhere or I should not have been trying to find some.

Q. You thought there were no sinkers at the farm to be had?

A. I thought there were no sinkers at the farm to be had.

Q. That is the reason you went into the second story of the barn to look for a sinker?

A. Yes sir.

Q. What made you think you would find sinkers there?

A. I heard father say, and I knew there was lead there.

Q. What made you think you would find sinkers there?

A. I went to see because there was lead there.

Q. You thought there might be lead there made into sinkers?

A. I thought there might be lead with a hole in it.

Q. Did you examine the lead that was downstairs near the door?

A. No sir.

Q. Why not?

A. I don't know.

Q. You went straight to the upper story of the barn?

A. No, I went under the pear tree and got some pears first.

Q. Then went to the second story of the barn to look for sinkers for lines you had at the farm, as you supposed, as you had seen them there five years before that time?

A. I went up to get some sinkers if I could find them. I did not intend to go to the farm for lines. I was going to buy some lines here.

Q. You then had no intention of using your lines at Marion?

A. I could not get them.

Q. You had no intention of using your own line and hooks at the farm?

A. No sir.

Q. What was the use of telling me a while ago you had no sinkers on your line at the farm?

A. I thought I made you understand that those lines at the farm were no good to use.

Q. Did you not mean for me to understand one of the reasons you were searching for sinkers was that the lines you had at the farm, as you remembered then, had no sinkers on them?

A. I said the lines at the farm had no sinkers.

Q. I did not ask you what you said. Did you not mean for me to understand that?

A. I meant for you to understand I wanted the sinkers and was going to have new lines.

Q. You had not then bought your lines?

A. No sir, I was going out Thursday noon.

Q. You had not bought any apparatus for fishing?

A. No hooks.

Q. Had bought nothing connected with your fishing trip?

A. No sir.

Q. Was going to go fishing the next Monday, were you?

A. I don't know that we should go fishing Monday.

Q. Going to the place to go fishing Monday?

A. Yes sir.

Q. This was Thursday and you had no idea of using any fishing apparatus before the next Monday?

A. No sir.

Q. You had no fishing apparatus you were proposing to use the next Monday until then?

A. No sir, not until I bought it.

Q. You had not bought anything?

A. No sir.

Q. Had you started to buy anything?

A. No sir.

Q. The first thing in preparation for your fishing trip the next Monday was to go to the loft of that barn to find some old sinkers to put on some hooks and lines that you had not then bought?

A. I thought if I found no sinkers, I would have to buy the sinkers when I bought the lines.

Q. You thought you would be saving something by hunting in the loft of the barn before you went to see whether you should need them or not?

A. I thought I would find out whether there were any sinkers before I bought the lines and if there was, I should not have to buy any sinkers. If there were some, I should only have to buy the lines and the hooks.

Q. You began the collection of your fishing apparatus by searching for the sinkers in the barn?

A. Yes sir.

Q. You were searching in a box of old stuff in the loft of the barn?

A. Yes sir, upstairs.

Q. That you had never looked at before?

A. I had seen them.

Q. Never examined them before?

A. No sir.

Q. All the reason you supposed there was sinkers there was your father had told you there was lead in the barn?

A. Yes, lead. And one day I wanted some old nails. He said there was some in the barn.

Q. All the reason that gave you to think there were sinkers was your father said there was old lead in the barn?

A. Yes sir.

Q. Did he mention the place in the barn?

A. I think he said upstairs. I'm not sure.

Q. Where did you look upstairs?

A. On that workbench like.

Q. In anything?

A. Yes. In a box---sort of a box. And then some things lying right on the side that was not in the box.

Q. How large a box was it?

A. I could not tell you. It was probably covered up---with lumber, I think.

Q. Give me the best idea of the size of the box you can.

A. Well, I should say I don't know. I have not any idea.

Q. Give me the best idea you have.

A. I have given you the best idea I have.

Q. What is the best idea you have?

A. About that large. (Measuring with her hands)

Q. That long?

A. Yes.

Q. How wide?

A. I don't know.

Q. Give me the best idea you have.

A. Perhaps about as wide as it was long.

Q. How high?

A. It was not very high.

Q. About how high?

A. (Witness measures with her hands).

Q. About twice the length of your forefinger?

A. I should think so. Not quite.

Q. What was in the box?

A. Nails and some old locks and I don't know but there was a doorknob.

Q. Anything else?

A. I don't remember anything else.

Q. Any lead?

A. Yes, some pieces of tea-lead like.

Q. Foil. What we call tinfoil; the same you use on tea chests?

A. I don't remember seeing any tinfoil, not as thin as that.

Q. Tea chest lead?

A. No sir.

Q. What did you see in shape of lead?

A. Flat pieces of lead a little bigger than that. Some of them were doubled together.

Q. How many?

A. I could not tell you.

Q. Where else did you look beside in the box?

A. I did not look anywhere for lead except on the workbench.

Q. How full was the box?

A. It was not nearly as full as it could have been.

Q. You looked on the bench. Beside that, where else?

A. Nowhere except on the bench.

Q. Did you look for anything else beside lead?

A. No sir.

Q. When you got through looking for lead, did you come down?

A. No sir. I went to the west window over the hay, to the west window, and the curtain was slanted a little. I pulled it down.

Q. What else?

A. Nothing.

Q. That is all you did?

A. Yes sir.

Q. That is the second story of the barn.

A. Yes sir.

Q. Was the window open?

A. I think not.

Q. Hot?

A. Very hot.

Q. How long do you think you were up there?

A. Not more than 15 or 20 minutes, I should not think.

Q. Should you think what you have told me would occupy four minutes?

A. Yes, because I ate some pears up there.

Q. Do you think all you have told me would take you four minutes?

A. I ate some pears up there.

Q. I asked you to tell me all you did.

A. I told you all I did.

Q. Do you mean to say you stopped your work and then, additional to that, sat still and ate some pears?

A. While I was looking out of the window, yes sir.

Q. Will you tell me all you did in the second story of the barn?

A. I think I told you all I did that I can remember.

Q. Is there anything else?

A. I told you that I took some pears up from the ground when I went up. I stopped under the pear tree and took some pears up when I went up.

Q. Have you now told me everything you did up in the second story of the barn?

A. Yes sir.

Q. I now call your attention and ask you to say whether all you have told me I don't suppose you stayed there any longer than was necessary?

A. No sir, because it was close.

Q. Can you give me any explanation why all you have told me would occupy more than three minutes?

A. Yes. It would take me more than three minutes.

# SHOCKING PSYCHIC SOLUTION:

Q. To look in that box that you have described the size of on the bench and put down the curtain and then get out as soon as you conveniently could; would you say you were occupied in that business 20 minutes?

A. I think so because I did not look at the box when I first went up.

Q. What did you do?

A. I ate my pears.

Q. Stood there eating the pears, doing nothing?

A. I was looking out of the window.

Q. Stood there looking out of the window, eating the pears?

A. I should think so.

Q. How many did you eat?

A. Three, I think.

Q. You were feeling better than you did in the morning?

A. Better than I did the night before.

Q. You were feeling better than you were in the morning?

A. I felt better in the morning than I did the night before.

Q. That is not what I asked you. You were then, when you were in that hayloft, looking out the window and eating three pears, feeling better, were you not, than you were in the morning when you could not eat any breakfast?

A. I never eat any breakfast.

Q. You did not answer my question and you will, if I have to put it all day. Were you then when you were eating those three pears in that hot loft, looking out that closed window, feeling better than you were in the morning when you ate no breakfast?

A. I was feeling well enough to eat the pears.

Q. Were you feeling better than you were in the morning?

# The Lizzie Borden Case

A. I don't think I felt very sick in the morning, only Yes, I don't know but I did feel better. As I say, I don't know whether I ate any breakfast or not or whether I ate a cookie.

Q. Were you then feeling better than you did in the morning?

A. I don't know how to answer you because I told you I felt better in the morning anyway.

Q. Do you understand my question? My question is whether, when you were in the loft of that barn, you were feeling better than you were in the morning when you got up?

A. No, I felt about the same.

Q. Were you feeling better than you were when you told your mother you did not care for any dinner?

A. No sir, I felt about the same.

Q. Well enough to eat pears, but not well enough to eat anything for dinner?

A. She asked me if I wanted any meat.

Q. I ask you why you should select that place, which was the only place which would put you out of sight of the house, to eat those three pears in?

A. I cannot tell you any reason.

Q. You observe that fact, do you not? You have put yourself in the only place, perhaps, where it would be impossible for you to see a person going into the house?

A. Yes sir, I should have seen them from the front window.

Q. From anywhere in the yard?

A. No sir, not unless from the end of the barn.

Q. Ordinarily in the yard you could see them and in the kitchen where you had been, you could have seen them?

A. I don't think I understand.

# SHOCKING PSYCHIC SOLUTION:

Q. When you were in the kitchen, you could see persons who came in at the back door?

A. Yes sir.

Q. When you were in the yard, unless you went around the corner of the house, you could see them come in at the back door?

A. No sir, not unless I was at the corner of the barn. The minute I turned, I could not.

Q. What was there?

A. A little jog, like. The walk turns.

Q. I ask you again to explain to me why you took those pears from the pear tree?

A. I did not take them from the pear tree.

Q. From the ground, wherever you took them from. I thank you for correcting me. Going into the barn, going upstairs into the hottest place in the barn, in the rear of the barn, the hottest place, and there standing and eating those pears that morning?

A. I beg your pardon. I was not in the rear of the barn. I was in the other end of the barn that faced the street.

Q. Where you could see anyone coming into the house?

A. Yes sir.

Q. Did you not tell me you could not?

A. Before I went into the barn---at the jog on the outside.

Q. You now say when you were eating the pears, you could see the back door?

A. Yes sir.

Q. So nobody could come in at that time without your seeing them?

A. I don't see how they could.

Q. After you got done eating your pears, you began your search?

A. Yes sir.

Q. Then you did not see into the house?

A. No sir, because the bench is at the other end.

Q. Now, I have asked you over and over again, and will continue the inquiry, whether anything you did at the bench would occupy more than three minutes?

A. Yes, I think it would because I pulled over quite a lot of boards in looking.

Q. To get at the box?

A. Yes sir.

Q. Taking all that, what is the amount of time you think you occupied in looking for that piece of lead which you did not find?

A. Well, I should think perhaps I was 10 minutes.

Q. Looking over those old things?

A. Yes sir, on the bench.

Q. Now can you explain why you were 10 minutes doing it?

A. No, only that I can't do anything in a minute.

Q. When you came down from the barn, what did you do then?

A. Came into the kitchen.

Q. What did you do then?

A. I went into the dining room and laid down my hat.

Q. What did you do then?

A. Opened the sitting room door and went into the sitting room; or pushed it open. It was not latched.

Q. What did you do then?

A. I found my father and rushed to the foot of the stairs.

Q. What were you going into the sitting room for?

A. To go upstairs.

Q. What for?

A. To sit down.

Q. What had become of the ironing?

A. The fire had gone out.

Q. I thought you went out because the fire was not hot enough to heat the flats.

A. I thought it would burn, but the fire had not caught from the few sparks.

Q. So you gave up the ironing and were going upstairs?

A. Yes sir, I thought I would wait till Maggie got dinner and heat the flats again.

Q. When you saw your father, where was he?

A. On the sofa.

Q. What was his position?

A. Lying down.

Q Describe anything else you noticed at that time.

A. I did not notice anything else, I was so frightened and horrified. I ran to the foot of the stairs and called Maggie.

Q. Did you notice that he had been cut?

A. Yes, that is what made me afraid.

Q. Did you notice that he was dead?

A. I did not know whether he was or not.

Q. Did you make any search for your mother?

A. No sir.

Q. Why not?

A. I thought she was out of the house. I thought she had gone out. I called Maggie to go to Dr. Bowen's. When they came in, I said, "I don't know where Mrs. Borden is." I thought she had gone out.

Q. Did you tell Maggie you thought your mother had come in?

A. No sir.

Q. That you thought you heard her come in?

A. No sir.

Q. Did you say to anybody that you thought she was killed upstairs?

A. No sir.

Q. To anybody?

A. No sir.

Q. You made no effort to find your mother at all?

A. No sir.

Q. Who did you send Maggie for?

A. Dr. Bowen. She came back and said Dr. Bowen was not there.

Q. What did you tell Maggie?

A. I told her he was hurt.

Q. When you first told her?

A. I says, "Go for Dr. Bowen as soon as you can. I think father is hurt."

Q. Did you then know that he was dead?

A. No sir.

Q. You saw him?

A. Yes sir.

Q. You went into the room?

A. No sir.

Q. Looked in at the door?

A. I opened the door and rushed back.

Q. Saw his face?

A. No, I did not see his face because he was all covered with blood.

Q. You saw where the face was bleeding?

A. Yes sir.

Q. Did you see the blood on the floor?

A. No sir.

Q. You saw his face covered with blood?

A. Yes sir.

Q. Did you see his eyeball hanging out?

A. No sir.

Q. See the gashes where his face was laid open?

A. No sir.

Q. Nothing of that kind?

A. No sir. (WITNESS COVERS HER FACE WITH HER HAND FOR A MINUTE OR TWO, THEN EXAMINATION IS RESUMED.)

Q. Do you know of any employment that would occupy your mother for the two hours between nine and 11 in the front room?

A. Not unless she was sewing.

Q. If she had been sewing you would have heard the machine.

A. She did not always use the machine.

Q. Did you see or were there found anything to indicate that she was sewing up there?

A. I don't know. She had given me a few weeks before some pillow cases to make.

Q. My question is not that. Did you see, or were there found, anything to indicate that she had done any sewing in that room that morning?

A. I don't know. I was not allowed in that room. I did not see it.

Q. Was that the room where she usually sewed?

A. No sir.

Q. Did you ever know of her using that room for sewing?

A. Yes sir.

Q. When?

A. Whenever she wanted to use the machine.

Q. When she did not want to use the machine, did you know she used that room for sewing?

A. Not unless she went up to sew a button on, or something.

Q. She did not use it as a sitting room?

A. No sir.

Q. Leaving out the sewing, do you know of anything else that would occupy her for two hours in that room?

A. No, not if she had made the bed up and she said she had when I went down.

Q. Assuming the bed was made?

A. I don't know anything.

Q. Did she say she had done the work?

A. She said she had made the bed and was going to put on the pillow cases, about 9 o'clock.

Q. I ask you now again, remembering that---.

A. I told you that yesterday.

Q. Never mind about yesterday. Tell me all the talk you had with your mother when she came down in the morning.

A. She asked me how I felt. I said I felt better but did not want any breakfast. She said what kind of meat did I want for dinner. I said I did not want any. She said she was going out; somebody was sick, and she would get the dinner, get the meat, order the meat. And I think she said something about the weather being hotter, or something; and I don't remember that she said anything else. I said to her, "Won't you change your dress before you go out?" She had on an old one. She said, "No, this is good enough." That is all I can remember.

Q. In this narrative you have not again said anything about her having said that she had made the bed.

A. I told you that she said she made the bed.

Q. In this time saying, you did not put that in. I want that conversation that you had with her that morning. I beg your pardon again. In this time of telling me, you did not say anything about her having received a note.

A. I told you that before.

Q. Miss Borden, I want you now to tell me all the talk you had with your mother when she came down, and all the talk she had with you. Please begin again.

A. She asked me how I felt. I told her. She asked me what I wanted for dinner. I told her not anything. What kind of meat I wanted for dinner. I told her not any. She said she had been up and made the spare bed and was going to take up some linen pillow cases for the small pillows at the foot and then the room was done. She says, "I have had a note from somebody that is sick and I am going out and I will get the dinner at the same time." I think she said something about the weather, I don't know. She also asked me if I would direct some paper wrappers for her, which I did.

Q. She said she had had a note?

A. Yes sir.

Q. You told me yesterday you never saw the note.

A. No sir, I never did.

Q. You looked for it?

A. No sir, but the rest have.

Q. She did not say where she was going?

A. No sir.

Q. Does she usually tell you where she is going?

A. She does not generally tell me.

Q. Did she say when she was coming back?

A. No sir.

Q. Did you know that Mr. Morse was coming to dinner?

A. No sir, I knew nothing about him.

Q. Was he at dinner the day before?

A. Wednesday noon? I don't know. I didn't see him. I don't think he was.

Q. Were you at dinner?

A. I was in the house. I don't know whether I went down to dinner or not. I was not feeling well.

Q. Whether you ate dinner or not?

A. I don't remember.

Q. Do you remember who was at dinner the day before?

A. No sir, I don't remember because I don't know whether I was down myself or not.

Q. Were you at tea Wednesday night?

A. I went down, but I think---I don't know---whether I had any tea or not.

Q. Did you sit down with the family?

A. I think I did, but I'm not sure.

Q. Was Mr. Morse there?

A. No sir, I did not see him.

Q. Who were there to tea?

A. Nobody.

Q. The family were there, I suppose.

A. Yes sir. I mean nobody but the family.

Q. Did you have an apron on Thursday?

A. Did I what?

Q. Have an apron on Thursday.

A. No sir, I don't think I did.

Q. Do you remember whether you did or not?

A. I don't remember for sure, but I don't think I did.

Q. You had aprons, of course?

A. I had aprons, yes sir.

Q. Will you try and think whether you did or not?

A. I don't think I did.

Q. Will you try and remember?

A. I had no occasion for an apron on that morning.

Q. If you can remember, I wish you would.

A. I don't remember.

Q. That is all the answer you can give me about that?

A. Yes sir.

Q. Did you have any occasion to use the axe or hatchet?

A. No sir.

Q. Did you know where they were?

A. I knew there was an old axe down cellar. That is all I knew.

Q. Did you know anything about a hatchet down cellar?

A. No sir.

Q. Where was the old axe down cellar?

A. The last time I saw it, it was stuck in the old chopping block.

Q. Was that the only axe or hatchet down cellar?

A. It was all I knew about.

Q. When was the last time you knew of it?

A. When our farmer came to chop wood.

Q. When was that?

A. I think a year ago last winter. I think there was so much wood on hand, he did not come last winter.

Q. Do you know of anything that would occasion the use of an axe or hatchet?

A. No sir.

Q. Do you know of anything that would occasion the getting of blood on an axe or hatchet down cellar?

A. No sir.

Q. I do not say there was, but assuming an axe or hatchet was found down cellar with blood on it?

A. No sir.

Q. Do you know whether there was a hatchet down there before this murder?

A. I don't know.

Q. You are not able to say your father did not own a hatchet?

A. I don't know whether he did or not.

Q. Did you know that there was found at the foot of the stairs a hatchet and axe?

A. No sir, I did not.

# SHOCKING PSYCHIC SOLUTION:

Q. Assume that is so, can you give me any explanation of how they came there?

A. No sir.

Q. Assume they had blood on them, can you give any occasion for there being blood on them?

A. No sir.

Q. Can you tell of the killing of any animal? Or any other operation that would lead to their being cast there, with blood on them?

A. No sir. He killed some pigeons in the barn last May or June.

Q. What with?

A. I don't know, but I thought he wrung their necks.

Q. What made you think so?

A. I think he said so.

Q. Did anything else make you think so?

A. All but three or four had their heads on. That is what made me think so.

Q. Did all of them come into the house?

A. I think so.

Q. Those that came into the house were all headless?

A. Two or three had them on.

Q. Were any with their heads off?

A. Yes sir.

Q. Cut off or twisted off?

A. I don't know which.

Q. How did they look?

A. I don't know, their heads were gone, that is all.

Q. Did you tell anybody they looked as though they were twisted off?

A. I don't remember whether I did or not. The skin, I think, was very tender. I said, "Why are these heads off?" I think I remember of telling somebody that he said they were twisted off.

Q. Did they look as if they were cut off?

A. I don't know. I did not look at that particularly.

Q. Is there anything else besides that that would lead, in your opinion so far as you can remember, to the finding of instruments in the cellar with blood on them?

A. I know of nothing else that was done.

Q. (By Judge Blaisdell) Was there any effort made by the witness to notify Mrs. Borden of the fact that Mr. Borden was found?

Q. (By Knowlton) Did you make any effort to notify Mrs. Borden of your father being killed?

A. No sir. When I found him, I rushed right to the foot of the stairs for Maggie. I supposed Mrs. Borden was out. I did not think anything about her at the time, I was so---.

Q. At any time, did you say anything about her to anybody?

A. No sir.

Q. To the effect that she was out?

A. I told father when he came in.

Q. After your father was killed?

A. No sir.

Q. Did you say you thought she was upstairs?

A. No sir.

Q. Did you ask them to look upstairs?

A. No sir.

Q. Did you suggest to anybody to search upstairs?

A. I said, "I don't know where Mrs. Borden is." That is all I said.

Q. You did not suggest that any search be made for her?

A. No sir.

Q. You did not make any yourself?

A. No sir.

Q. I want you to give me all that you did, by way of word or deed, to see whether your mother was dead or not, when you found your father was dead.

A. I did not do anything except what I said to Mrs. Churchill. I said to her, "I don't know where Mrs. Borden is. I think she is out, but I wish you would look."

Q. You did ask her to look?

A. I said that to Mrs. Churchill.

Q. Where did you intend for her to look?

A. In Mrs. Borden's room.

Q. When you went out to the barn, did you leave the door shut, the screen door?

A. I left it shut.

Q. When you came back did you find it shut or open?

A. No sir, I found it open.

Q. Can you tell me anything else that you did that you have not told me, during your absence from the house?

A. No sir.

Q. Can you tell me when it was that you came back from the barn, what time it was?

A. I am not sure, but I think it must have been after 10, because I think he told me he did not think he should go out until 10.

When he went out, I did not look at the clock to see what time it was. I think he did not go out until 10, or a little after. He was not gone so very long.

Q. Will you give me the best judgment you can as to the time your father got back? If you have not any, it is sufficient to say so.

A. No sir, I have not any.

Q. Can you give me any judgment as to the length of time that elapsed after he came back and before you went to the barn?

A. I went right out to the barn.

Q. How soon after he came back?

A. I should think not less than five minutes. I saw him taking off his shoes and lying down. It only took him two or three minutes to do it. I went right out.

Q. When he came into the house, did he not go into the dining room first?

A. I don't know.

Q. And there sit down?

A. I don't know.

Q. Why don't you know?

A. Because I was in the kitchen.

Q. It might have happened and you not have known it?

A. Yes sir.

Q. You heard the bell ring?

A. Yes sir.

Q. And you knew when he came in?

A. Yes sir.

Q. You did not see him?

A. No sir.

# SHOCKING PSYCHIC SOLUTION:

Q. When did you first see him?

A. I went into the sitting room and he was there. I don't know whether he had been in the dining room before or not.

Q. What made you go into the sitting room?

A. Because I wanted to ask him a question.

Q. What question?

A. Whether there was any mail for me.

Q. Did you not ask him that question in the dining room?

A. No sir, I think not,

Q. Was he not in the dining room sitting down?

A. I don't remember his being in the dining room sitting down.

Q. At that time, was not Maggie washing the windows in the sitting room?

A. I thought I asked him for the mail in the sitting room. I am not sure.

Q. Was not the reason he went into the dining room because she was in the sitting room washing windows?

A. I don't know.

Q. Did he not go upstairs to his room before he sat down in the sitting room?

A. I did not see him go.

Q. He had the key to his room down there?

A. I don't know whether he had it. It was kept on the shelf.

Q. Don't you remember he took the key and went into his own room and then came back?

A. No sir.

Q. You don't remember anything of that kind?

A. No sir. I do not think he did go upstairs either.

Q. You will swear he did not?

A. I did not see him.

Q. You swear you did not see him?

A. Yes sir.

Q. You were either in the kitchen or sitting room all the time?

A. Yes sir.

Q. He could not have gone up without he had gone through the kitchen?

A. No sir.

Q. When you did go into the sitting room to ask him a question, if it was the sitting room, what took place then?

A. I asked him if he had any mail. He said, "None for you." He had a letter in his hand. I supposed it was for himself. I asked him how he felt. He said, "About the same." He said he should lie down. I asked him if he thought he should have a nap. He said he should try to. I asked him if he wanted the window left the way it was or if he felt a draught. He said, "No." That is all.

Q. Did you help him about lying down?

A. No sir.

Q. Fix his pillows or head?

A. No sir. I did not touch the sofa.

Q. Did he lie down before you left the room?

A. Yes sir.

Q. Did anything else take place?

A. Not that I remember of.

Q. Was he then under medical treatment?

A. No sir.

Q. The doctor had not given him any medicine that you know of?

# SHOCKING PSYCHIC SOLUTION:

A. No sir. He took some medicine; it was not doctor's medicine. It was what we gave him.

Q. What was it?

A. We gave him castor oil first and then Garfield tea.

Q. When was that?

A. He took the castor oil some time Wednesday. I think some time Wednesday noon and I think the tea Wednesday night. Mrs. Borden gave it to him. She went over to see the doctor.

Q. When did you first consult Mr. Jennings?

A. I can't tell you that. I think my sister sent for him. I don't know.

Q. Was it you or your sister?

A. My sister.

Q. You did not send for him?

A. I did not send for him. She said did we think we should have him. I said do as she thought best. I don't know when he came first.

Q. Now, tell me once more, if you please, the particulars of that trouble that you had with your mother four or five years ago.

A. Her father's house on Ferry Street was for sale-...

Q. Whose father's house?

A. Mrs. Borden's father's house. She had a stepmother and a half-sister, Mrs. Borden did, and this house was left to the stepmother and a half-sister, if I understand it right, and the house was for sale. The stepmother, Mrs. Oliver Gray, wanted to sell it and my father bought out the Widow Gray's share. She did not tell me and he did not tell me, but some outsiders said he gave it to her, put it in her name. I said if he gave that to her, he ought to give us something. Told Mrs. Borden so. She did not care anything about the house herself. She wanted it so this half-sister could have a home because she had married a man that was not doing the best he could and she thought her sister was having a very hard time and wanted her to have a home. And we always thought she persuaded father to buy it. At any rate, he did buy it and I am quite sure she did persuade him. I said what he did for her, he ought to do for his own children. So, he gave us grandfather's house. That was all the trouble we ever had.

Q. You have not stated any trouble yet between you and her.

A. I said there was feeling four or five years ago when I stopped calling her mother. I told you that yesterday.

Q. That is all there is to it then?

A. Yes sir.

Q. You had no words with your stepmother then?

A. I talked with her about it and said what he did for her, he ought to do for us. That is all the words we had.

Q. That is the occasion of his giving you the house that you sold back to him?

A. Yes sir.

Q. Did your mother leave any property?

A. I don't know.

Q. Your own mother?

A. No sir, not that I know of.

Q. Did you ever see that thing? (Pointing to a wooden club)

A. Yes, I think I have.

Q. What is it?

A. My father used to keep something similar to this, that looked very much like it, under his bed. He whittled it out himself at the farm one time.

Q. How long since you have seen it?

A. I have not seen it in years.

## SHOCKING PSYCHIC SOLUTION:

Q. How many years?

A. I could not tell you. I should think 10 or 15 years. Not since I was quite a little girl, if that is the one. I can't swear that it is the one. It was about that size.

Q. (Marks it with a cross) How many years, 10 or 15?

A. I was a little girl. It must have been as much as that.

Q. When was the last time the windows were washed before that day?

A. I don't know.

Q. Why don't you know?

A. Because I had nothing to do with the work downstairs.

Q. When was the last time that you ate with the family that you can swear to before your mother was killed?

A. Well, I ate with them all day Tuesday. That is, what little we ate. We sat down at the table and I think I sat down to the table with them Wednesday night, but I am not sure.

Q. All day Tuesday?

A. I was down at the table.

Q. I understand you to say you did not come down to breakfast.

A. That was Wednesday morning.

Q. I understood you to say that you did not come down to breakfast.

A. I came down but I did not eat breakfast with them. I did not eat any breakfast. Frequently, I would go into the dining room and sit down to the table with them and not eat any breakfast.

Q. Did you give to the officer the same skirt you had on the day of the tragedy?

A. Yes sir.

Q. Do you know whether there was any blood on the skirt?

A. No sir.

Q. Assume that there was, do you know how it came there?

A. No sir.

Q. Have you any explanation of how it might come there?

A. No sir.

Q. Did you know there was any blood on the skirt you gave them?

A. No sir.

Q. Assume that there was. Can you give any explanation of how it came there on the dress skirt?

A. No sir.

Q. Have you offered any?

A. No sir.

Q Have you ever offered any?

A. No sir.

Q. Have you said it came from fleabites?

A. On the petticoats, I said there was a fleabite. I said it might have been. You said you meant the dress skirt.

Q. I did. Have you offered any explanation how that came there?

A. I told those men that were at the house that I had had fleas. That is all.

Q. Did you offer that as an explanation?

A. I said that was the only explanation that I knew of.

Q. Assuming that the blood came from the outside, can you give any explanation of how it came there?

A. No sir.

Q. You cannot now?

A. No sir.

## SHOCKING PSYCHIC SOLUTION:

Q. What shoes did you have on that day?

    A. A pair of ties.

Q. What color?

    A. Black.

Q. Will you give them to the officer?

    A. Yes.

Q. Where are they?

    A. At home.

Q. What stockings did you have on that day?

    A. Black.

Q. Where are they?

    A. At home.

Q. Have they been washed?

    A. I don't know.

Q. Will you give them to the officer?

    A. Yes sir.

Q. The window you were at is the window that is nearest the street in the barn?

    A. Yes sir, the west window.

Q. The pears you ate you got from under the tree in the yard?

    A. Yes sir.

Q. How long were you under the pear tree?

    A. I think I was under there very nearly four or five minutes. I stood looking around. I looked up at the pigeon house that they have closed up. It was no more than five minutes, perhaps not as long. I can't say sure.

Q. (By Judge Blaisdell) Was this witness on Thursday morning in the front hall of front stairs or front chamber, any part of the house at all?

Q. What do you say to that?

A. I had to come down the front stairs to get into the kitchen.

Q. When you came down first?

A. Yes sir.

Q. Were you afterwards?

A. No sir.

Q. Not at all?

A. Except the few minutes I went up with the clean clothes and I had to come back again.

Q. That you now say was before Mr. Borden went away?

A. Yes sir.

(HEARING ADJOURNED. LIZZIE BORDEN RECALLED AUGUST 11th)

Q. Is there anything you would like to correct in your previous testimony?

A. No sir.

Q. Did you buy a dress pattern in New Bedford?

A. A dress pattern?

Q. Yes.

A. I think I did.

Q. Where is it?

A. It is at home.

Q. Where?

A. Where at home?

Q. Please.

A. It is in a trunk.

Q. In your room?

A. No sir, in the attic.

Q. Not made up?

A. Oh, no sir.

Q. Where did you buy it?

A. I don't know the name of the store.

Q. On the principal street there?

A. I think it was on the street that Hutchinson's bookstore is on. I am not positive.

Q. What kind of a one was it, please?

A. It was a pink stripe and a white stripe and a blue stripe corded gingham.

Q. Your attention has already been called to the circumstances of going into the drug store of Smith's on the corner of Columbia and Main Streets, by some officer, has it not, on the day before the tragedy?

A. I don't know whether some officer has asked me. Somebody has spoken of it to me. I don't know who it was.

Q. Did that take place?

A. It did not.

Q. Do you know where the drugstore is?

A. I don't.

Q. Did you go into any drugstore and inquire for prussic acid?

A. I did not.

Q. Where were you on Wednesday morning that you remember?

A. At home.

Q. All the time?

A. All day, until Wednesday night.

Q. Nobody there but your parents and yourself and the servant?

A. Why, Mr. Morse came sometime in the afternoon, or at noontime, I suppose. I did not see him.

Q. He did not come to see you?

A. No sir. I did not see him.

Q. He did not come until afternoon anyway, did he?

A. I don't think he did. I'm not sure.

Q. Did you dine with the family that day?

A. I was downstairs, yes sir. I did not eat any breakfast with them.

Q. Did you go into the drugstore for any purpose whatever?

A. I did not.

Q. I think you said yesterday that you did not go into the room where your father lay, after he was killed, on the sofa, but only looked in at the door.

A. I looked in. I did not go in.

Q. You did not step into the room at all?

A. I did not.

Q. Did you ever, after your mother was found killed, any more than go through it to go upstairs?

A. When they took me upstairs, they took me through that room.

Q. Otherwise than that, did you go into it?

A. No sir.

Q. Let me refresh your memory. You came down in the night to get some water with Miss Russell, along towards night, or in the evening, to get some water with Miss Russell?

# SHOCKING PSYCHIC SOLUTION:

A. Thursday night? I don't remember it.

Q. Don't you remember coming down some time to get some toilet water?

A. No sir. There was no toilet water downstairs.

Q. Or to empty the slops?

A. I don't know whether I did Thursday evening or not. I am not sure.

Q. You think it may have been some other evening?

A. I don't remember coming down with her to do such a thing. I may have. I can't tell whether it was Thursday evening or any other evening.

Q. Other than that, if it did take place, you don't recollect going into that room for any purpose at any time?

A. No sir.

Q. Was the dress that was given the officers the same dress that you wore that morning?

A. Yes sir.

Q. The India silk?

A. No sir. It is not an India silk. It is silk and linen. Some call it Bengaline silk.

Q. Something like that dress there? (Pongee)

A. No, it was not like that.

Q. Did you give to the officer the same shoes and stockings that you wore?

A. I did, sir.

Q. Do you remember where you took them off?

A. I wore the shoes ever after that, all around the house Friday and all day Thursday and all day Friday and Saturday until I put on my shoes for the street.

Q. That is to say you wore them all that day, Thursday, until you took them off for the night?

A. Yes sir.

Q. Did you tell us yesterday all the errands that you had at the barn?

A. Yes sir.

Q. You have nothing to add to what you said?

A. No sir.

Q. Miss Borden, of course you appreciate the anxiety that everybody has to find the author of this tragedy, and the questions that I put to you have been in that direction. I now ask you if you can furnish any other fact, or give any other, even suspicion, that will assist the officers in any way in this matter.

A. About two weeks ago---.

Q. Were you going to tell the occurrence about the man that called at the house?

A. No sir. It was after my sister went away. I came home from Miss Russell's one night and as I came up, I always glanced towards the side door. As I came along by the carriageway, I saw a shadow on the side steps. I did not stop walking, but I walked slower. Somebody ran down the steps, around the east end of the house. I thought it was a man because I saw no skirts and I was frightened, and, of course, I did not go around to see. I hurried in the front door as fast as I could and locked it.

Q. What time of the night was that?

A. I think about a quarter of 9. It was not after 9 o'clock, anyway.

Q. Do you remember what night that was?

A. No sir, I don't. I saw somebody run around the house once before last winter.

Q. One thing at a time. Do you recollect about how long that occurrence was?

A. It was after my sister went away. She has been away two weeks today, so it must have been within two weeks.

Q. Two weeks today? Or two weeks at the time of the murder?

A. Is not today Thursday?

A. Yes, but that would be three weeks. I thought you said the day your father was murdered, she had been away just two weeks.

A. Yes, she had.

Q. Then, it would be three weeks today your sister went away. A week has elapsed.

A. Yes, it would be three weeks.

Q. You mean it was some time within the two weeks that your sister was away?

A. Yes. I had forgotten that a whole week had passed since the affair.

Q. Different from that, you cannot state?

A. No sir. I don't know what the date was.

Q. This form, when you first saw it, was on the steps of the backdoor?

A. Yes sir.

Q. Went down the rear steps?

A. Went down toward the barn.

Q. Around the back side of the house?

A. Disappeared in the dark. I don't know where they went.

Q. Have you ever mentioned that before?

A. Yes sir, I told Mr. Jennings.

Q. To any officer?

A. I don't think I have, unless I told Mr. Hanscomb.

Q. What were you going to say about last winter?

A. Last winter when I was coming home from church one Thursday evening, I saw somebody run around the house again. I told my father of that.

Q. Did you tell your father of this last one?

A. No sir.

Q. Of course you could not identify who it was either time?

A. No, I could not identify who it was, but it was not a very tall person.

Q. Have you sealskin sacks?

A. Yes sir.

Q. Where are they?

A. Hanging in a large white bag in the attic, each one separate.

Q. Put away for the summer?

A. Yes sir.

Q. Do you ever use prussic acid on your sacks?

A. Acid? No sir, I don't use anything on them.

Q. Is there anything else you can suggest that even amounts to anything whatever?

A. I know of nothing else, except the man who came and father ordered him out. That is all I know.

Q. That you told about the other day?

A. I think I did, yes sir.

Q. You have not been able to find that man?

A. I have not. I don't know whether anybody else has or not.

Q. Have you caused search to be made for him?

# Shocking Psychic Solution:

A. Yes sir.

Q. When was the offer of reward made for the detection of the criminals?

A. I think it was made Friday.

Q. Who suggested that?

A. We suggested it ourselves and asked Mr. Buck if he did not think it was a good plan.

Q. Whose suggestion was it, yours or Emma's?

A. I don't remember. I think it was mine.


## (THE EXAMINATION ENDED)

# APPENDIX THREE
# THE LIZZIE BORDEN BED AND BREAKFAST

92 Second Street
Fall River, MA 02721
Phone: 508-675-7333 Fax 508-673-1541
Web site: www.Lizzie-Borden.com
The Lizzie Borden Home now a Bed and Breakfast

Our beautifully restored Greek-revival home is now a first-class bed & breakfast. You are invited to choose one of 6 beautifully appointed bedrooms and roam the house to learn the true facts. What were the thoughts of the first police officers on the scene? Who were the suspects? What was the public's

reaction? Will you join the legions who think Lizzie guilty, or will you choose to be a stalwart defender?

In the morning we invite you to enjoy a hot breakfast reminiscent of the food the Borden's ate on that fateful Thursday in 1892.

For a unique experience, be our guest for an evening ...Lizzie awaits you.

Please visit our MySpace page at www.MySpace.com/LizzieBordenBB

# Shocking Psychic Solution:

**Tours of the house** 11 a.m. to 3 p.m. Photographs are permitted
Tickets $10 Adults, $8 Sr. Citizens, $5 Children 2 to 12 years of age.
Reservations are preferred.

**Room rates**: (subject to change at any time—some discounts for out of season)
  Abby's Dressing Room   $250
  Andrew Borden's Bedroom $250
  Emma Borden's Bedroom $225
  John Morse Bedroom (Abby' death site) $225
  Lizzie Borden's Bedroom   $225
  Bridget Sullivan's Attic Bedroom (single) $175

**Lizzie Borden Gift Shop**
  Mugs with house picture $5
  Mugs with Lizzie Borden image $5
  Hatchet Earrings (silver) $5
  Phantom Cat statues $25
  Lizzie Borden Baseball Cap. $20
  I survived the night at Lizzie Borden House T-shirt $20
  Lizzie Borden T-Shirt (portrait) $20
  Lizzie Borden Bobble head doll $20
  Brick dust from Haunted Basement $10.

# APPENDIX FOUR
# GHOST STORIES LINKED TO THE
# LIZZIE BORDEN HOUSE B&B.

Guides on the tour of the house tell of many strange events happenings. The cellar is believed to be very haunted. They say that things in the house go missing, only to turn up again after a time (a classic "aport"). Visitors have been touched by unseen hands in the house and those who have spent a night in the home tell of encountering a phantom woman in a Victorian dress dusting (perhaps the ghost of Abby). Others have heard a weeping woman in the rooms. One of the stranger stories feature a woman in an old style dress tucking people in bed late at night.

Footsteps are heard throughout the house and on the stairs. When people check, there is no one there to account for the sounds. Emma's Room seems to be the center of supernatural activity with one reporter recording a phantom woman's laugh one night after a séance. Beds become rumpled right after they were made, only to be re-made by phantom hands. Doors in the house open and close, seemingly on their own. Many visitors who claim to have a psychic gift believe that the place is haunted by the spirits of Abby and Andrew, the victims of the crime. Perhaps the oddest ghosts are that of spectral cats felt by visitors. They have felt cats jump on the bed at night, walk over to them and roll up next to them as if to sleep—when they turn on the light there is nothing there. There are no cats at the house today. Lights flicker in this house and camera batteries are drained of power from time to time. The flickering of the lights is believed to be an indication that ghosts are present. Visit the house and spend a night. Perhaps you will encounter the ghost of Lizzie Borden and you can ask her personally what happened that hot August day in 1892.

The Borden House at 92 Second Street & the barn at the rear,
where Lizzie claimed to be during the murders

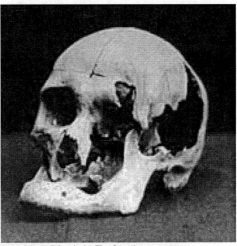

Andrew Borden (Lizzie's Father)

Andrew Borden (Lizzie's Father)

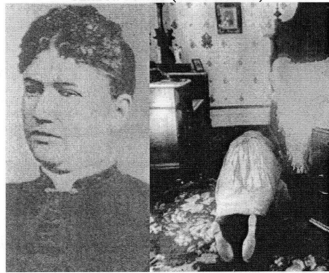

Abbie Borden (Lizzie's Mother)

# Shocking Psychic Solution:

Actress Nance O'Neil,
with whom it has been rumored that Lizzie had a long affair.

The Borden's maid,
Bridget Sullivan

Emma Lenora Borden
(Lizzie's Sister)

# Appendix Five
# Ghost Research

Photo by Guy W. Kitchens

Richard Senate at the Bella Maggiore Inn.

PAUL WELLMAN

Ghost stalker Richard Senate sits on the steps of the Victorian Rose Inn, one of the South Coast's most haunted spots.

# Is There a Ghost in the House?

## Uncovering the Unknown with Ghost Stalker Richard Senate

### by Matt Kettmann

**D**o you know any ghost stories? I do. Plenty, in fact, and every time I tell one, be it to a friend or stranger, I always get one in return. Usually, it's a second-hand rendition, likely enhanced for dramatic effect in lieu of from the observer's mouth. But other times, the stories come straight from the observer's mouth, often in a slightly guarded tone, as if the particular ghost might be within earshot.

The prevalence of such stories only leads me to believe that ghosts must exist. In fact, I think I have one or two in my house, having one night caught a glimpse of a little boy on my back porch, and occasionally hearing voices.

People are fascinated by such tales, as much as I am when I hear my friends' tales about a run-in with a girl ghost in Los Olivos; or how a football team ran full-speed from rustling bushes in Fillmore; or how they once saw a floating image in their childhood bedroom. When the window washers go on in my car unexpectedly, I like to tell people there's a ghost in there, too.

Considering few of us have ever experienced a ghostly phenomenon, apparitions play an amazingly prevalent role in our society. We're indoctrinated with ghost stories around campfires as kids, spend part of our adolescent years investigating places we've heard to be haunted, gather our own repertoire of ghastly tales throughout college, and then slowly slip into a casual yet cautious denial of their existence as we get older—unless, of course, we see one ourselves. As one friend once said to me, "You'll probably only know everything about ghosts when you become one."

But thanks to the progress of modern science—specifically the field of metaphysics as it uncovers the inner workings of energy and the not-so-linear reality of time—there may be an explanation for the odd occurrences attributed to ghosts just around the corner. That corner could be decades away,

but for the first time since the advent of Newtonian physics, science—that broad field that skeptics have always depended upon to shoot down the "crazy" idea of spirits—is opening the doors for the paranormal.

## Ghost Stalker Extraordinaire

When Halloween comes 'round—and concurrently, the Day of the Dead (Día de los Muertos) and other cultural manifestations of afterlife celebration—we become transfixed with ghosts. Kids put on sheets and say "Boo!" Horror movies sell out repeatedly. Haunted houses pop up on every other corner. Television shows highlight "unsolved mysteries," the "most haunted hotels of America," and "how to catch a ghost."

Here at *The Independent*, we decided to join in the fun, so I called up Richard Senate, a City of Ventura historian by day and world-renowned ghost stalker by night. Author of nearly one dozen books on where to find ghosts in Southern California and beyond, Senate also runs a web site (*www.ghost-stalker.com*) that gets close to 200 hits per day from users as far away as China and Norway. Add to that being a consultant for numerous TV shows and movies, it's no wonder Senate has become one of the world's favorite contacts for owners of haunted houses and witnesses of otherworldly visions.

Last Friday afternoon I met Senate at his office in the marbled Ventura City Hall. We walked a few blocks through downtown Ventura toward the Victorian Rose Inn, a church built in 1888 that was recently converted into a bed-and-breakfast. As he gave a tour of the ornately decorated, five-bedroom inn—where the preponderance and eerie detail of ghostly occurrences Senate related had me jumping at the sounds of a creaking door and brushes of a bed skirt—he intermixed his personal history with his philosophical understanding of the ghost world.

His interest in ghosts was sparked by an incident more than 20 years ago. When doing archaeology work late one night at the San Antonio de Padua Mission near King City, Senate became hungry and started to walk across the courtyard from his office to the kitchen. On his way, he saw a monk passing through—a regular happening as the mission was still a monastery—and went up to say hi. As Senate got within a few feet, the monk, which was as "solid as a regular person, not wispy or anything," vanished. "I wasn't smoking anything or drinking anything funny," Senate assured. He immediately began looking for the hole that the monk had fallen into, then realized he'd just seen his first ghost, and went to bed without supper but with the light on. Although slightly freaked out, he made the decision about "30 seconds" after he'd seen the apparition to start a lifelong investigation of ghosts.

For a man who's visited more than 250 haunted places and been involved in close to 100 séances—a tally that would lead many to expect a New Age, crystal-carrying guru type or, alternately, a black-clothes-wearing minister-type with deep foreboding voice—Senate is remarkably sensible and even funny when he discusses the paranormal. He's only seen about 15 ghosts himself in his 25 years of work, an almost embarrassingly modest number that, at least in my eyes, affirms his credibility as an agent of truth rather than a tall-tale-spinning opportunist.

Senate gets a handful of calls each day about hauntings, possible poltergeists, and unexplained experiences. And he said that while he believes ghosts are common, he doesn't stop people from lying about them. Luckily, he's learned how to cull the fakes from the true hauntings, explaining, "Real ghosts tend to be boring. They're nothing like the movie ghosts."

Like everyday living humans, ghosts typically do relatively mundane things, such as walking through a room, rocking in a chair, or just standing around. That they happen to go through walls and disappear—or, occasionally, do some-

Ghost continued on p. 35▶

thing mischievous like move socks, hide keys, or pile a restaurant's tables on top of each other—is usually what prompts someone to call. And from those calls, Senate has compiled an extensive library of his own works. The collection includes fun-reading ghost hunts that range from *The Ghosts of the Haunted Coast*, a 1986 publication that features an entire section on the ghosts of Santa Barbara County, to *Hollywood's Ghosts*, which was published this month and is, according to Senate, "selling like hotcakes."

But what makes Senate most believable in a field many assume is full of wackos is his openness to explanations about what ghosts actually are. "I don't know what ghosts are," Senate said. "I'm trying to find out. I assume it's something very complicated. Only about 20 percent have any correlation with actual dead people. The other 80 percent are a complete mystery."

Perhaps they're bends in the fabric of time, he suggested, so that when we see ghosts, we're actually looking back in time for a split second. Or maybe, when undergoing extreme trauma, we project an "emotional trace" into our surroundings, leaving some unbound energy to "haunt" a room or house after we're dead. Or maybe ghosts are glimpses into parallel dimensions, realms we haven't the slightest clue about but that modern science has predicted can feasibly exist. And though he didn't say this—perhaps because he's often attacked by religious types for spreading news about the devil—I got the sense that Senate is so open to theories that he may even entertain a spiritual explanation of unfinished business or being stuck in some afterlife limbo.

In any case, talking about what ghosts are is only part of the fun. Senate is quite clear of *what* ghosts might be, so I just had to ask: *Where* are they in Santa Barbara?

# Do the Walk of Haunts

Since *The Ghosts of the Haunted Coast* was published in 1986, Senate has come upon scores more stories of haunted places in Santa Barbara County. He's got another South Coast book up his sleeve, but until it's published, we're left with a collection of well-known stories, unfounded rumors, and conjecture. The most interesting haunts happen to be in private residences, but we're not privy to publish those addresses, nor would the owners want a longer trick-or-treat line than normal. So what follows may not be the most haunted places of Santa Barbara, but at least they are the ones we can see from a distance.

Perhaps the most famous on the entire South Coast is Hector of Summerland's Big Yellow House. While the current management claims that the only funny stuff that happens occurs after drinking Irish whiskey into the wee hours, older stories tell of tables rearranged overnight, electrical switches with their own agenda, and windows that would rather be open than closed. In perhaps one of his most memorable experiences, Senate recalled a séance there when a tape recorder flew across the room, smashed into the wall, and then spit the tape out all over the floor.

There are also stories from the many old businesses on lower State Street—from Joe's Café to Pier One Imports, which recently put in a call to Senate— where voices, moving things, and mysterious figures abound. The third story of Q's Sushi A Go-Go is rumored to be haunted, and given its reported past as a brothel, such claims are likely to be true. Though he hadn't heard about Q's, Senate confirmed that many old brothels are haunted, often filled with female laughter and general revelry.

As for haunted hotels, try the Upham, where William Henry Dana supposedly wrote *Two Years Before the Mast*. There's a desk there that some say is haunted by his ghost. Or the San Ysidro Ranch, where onetime owner Ronald Coleman is still seen walking the grounds or sitting at the bar.

Many claim that St. Francis Hospital was haunted by a monk who helped people get into the afterlife. "Apparently he wasn't that good of a guide," joked Senate, "because he was usually seen wandering aimlessly, and once even hovering around the second floor."

Then there's the Old Mission, the Presidio, and Casa de la Guerra, where people have been living and dying for centuries. I've heard a few good ones about the outskirts of the Presidio, and, as my house is on the Presidio grounds, the experiences I've had would fall under its flag. Senate told me that the Santa Barbara Mission is most certainly haunted by at least one ghost, though not quite as many as La Purísima Mission near Lompoc, the "capital of the ghosts," where nine separate apparitions have been reported.

And up that way, past a newly noticed haunting at an abandoned Civil War cemetery off of Painted Cave Road, there's also the ghost of Cold Spring Tavern. But it's in the bar, not the restaurant, because, as Senate explained, "Spirits tend to like spirits."

That's the short list. There are plenty more haunted places in an old town such as ours, but you'll have to find them yourself. Thankfully, this Halloween weekend, there are two tours to help you out. The **First Annual Haunted Trolley Ghost Tour**, which Senate helped organize, leaves at 7 p.m. from Stearns Wharf every night until November 2. $15. Call 965-0353. Then there's **Santa Barbara's Haunted History Tours**, starting Halloween night at 6, 7:30, and 9 p.m., at 628 State St. $15. Call 746-2166. ∎

In his 25 years of hunting ghosts, Senate has visited more than 250 haunted places and organized close to 100 séances. In all those experiences though, he's only seen 15 or so ghosts with his own eyes.

Richard Senate and Psychic Chris Fleming
(Taping the DeadFamous Television Show)

# Family

# Chasing ghosts

## Family attempts to call up spirits

By Stephanie Bertholdo
bertholdo@theacorn.com

Is the historic Reyes Adobe rancho in Agoura Hills haunted?

Richard Senate, a well-known ghost hunter, author and lecturer, deemed the 1850s house and barn haunted Sunday night when he conducted a tour and ghost hunt for 19 people—including me.

After recounting ghost tales of California's missions and telling spooky stories in the dark, Senate, his psychic wife, Debbie, and daughter Megan, 16, handed out divining rods to guests to try to lure out ghostly spirits who may still lurk in the home after 156 years.

They also used digital cameras and other electronic gadgets to capture disembodied voices and static electrical variations in the rooms—all possible signatures of a ghost.

The teenagers on the tour got into the spirit. They took turns using the dowsing rods made from coat hangers, and seemed to channel a few ghostly spirits who "answered" yes and no questions through the swaying rods. The bent ends of the dowsing rods were used as handles; and when queried, the two wires either stayed still for "yes," or crossed over with a "no" response.

One or two ghosts supposedly reside in the home, and an Oak Park High School student, Richie Warmus, said he had seen a face in the barn window. Debbie Senate told the boy he was just seeing a piece of paper in the window, but when they peered toward the barn again, the paper?—and the face?—were gone.

Although I consider myself a skeptic on all things supernatural, I experienced something strange at the home. As the kids took turns with the dowsing rods, I stood at the foot of the stairs looking down at the ground when Senate suggested taking a trip to the upper level. I thought I'd be the first person to climb to the second story. In a split second, a snakelike, partially vaporous white light—with a bit of substance to it—squirmed and shot through a square hole at the base of the stairs.

Do I believe this light was the beginning of a ghostly manifestation? I just know what it wasn't—it wasn't a light from a flashlight because it appeared three-dimensional and no one with a flashlight was standing near me. It wasn't a figment of my imagination—I was finding the whole experience a bit funny, rather than scary, so I had not fallen into a state where I could be considered "ripe" for such an experience. I simply have no explanation for the light.

"When I first came I was kind of skeptical, and I wasn't expecting much," said Sharon Wu, a 16-year-old Oak Park High School student. "But there was a lot of tension in the room . . . and I got really scared."

Diane Olmstead, 49, of Moorpark said she wasn't sure she was a true believer but liked the way the hunt opened up the possibility of ghosts amongst us.

Brianna Fischer, a 15-year-old who handled the dowsing rods in the house, said she had always believed in ghosts. She said she tried to keep the dowsing rod still, but couldn't control its movement.

Paul Fremeau, a junior at Oak Park High, backed her up. "They moved by themselves," he said.

# in the Reyes Adobe rancho

MARIA McGINLEY/Special to The Acorn

**GHOSTBUSTERS**—Richard Senate, left, is an established ghost hunter in California. He's pictured with his wife, psychic Debbie Senate, and their 16-year-old daughter, Megan. After investigating the historic Reyes Adobe on Sunday the Senates report the rancho is haunted by at least two ghosts.

Richard Senate is helping drive tourism in Ventura with his tours and books about haunted locales. The bell tower at the San Buenaventura Mission is one location said to have its own ghost.

# Haunting appeal

# Forget 'Blair Witch.' For something really scary, Richard Senate has the place

Having seen "The Blair Witch Project" over the weekend and then wanting to see something really scary, I decided to check out area ghost hunter Richard Senate's Web site at *http://www.ghost-stalker.com*.

Senate is known throughout the area and across the state as a man set on uncovering the truth about ghosts.

Like the three castaways who set out to uncover the truth about the title character in "Blair Witch," Senate has on many occasions gone after apparitions. But instead of incessant whining and worrying about things that go slime in the night, Senate approaches his work in a different fashion than his "Blair Witch" counterparts, summed up by the man himself as "a sane approach to the investigation of ghosts and paranormal activity."

The "Blair Witch" gang could have taken a cue from the ghost stalker.

From the start, Senate packs realism into his site. The first section you click on tells of Senate's birth in LA, childhood in Venice and winters in Thousand Oaks where he may have had his first encounter with a ghost — in a barn.

"A friend of the family said that he heard ghosts there," Senate said. "He called out to them thinking some of his friends were there, but there was nothing, only phantom voices and shadows.

"I been talkin' to spooks'! I recall him say-

ing whenever he told of the event, and I heard the story many times while growing up."

Buried within Senate's spooky site are sections called "Ghosts We Have Stalked," "Tales From Tombstones" and "Tales From Beneath the Sod" all packed with stories galore.

The section that you won't want to miss is "Richard Senate's Ghost Gallery," where you can see photos of 'ghostly apparitions Richard Senate has acquired in his career as a professional ghost hunter." You can see the ghost in the graveyard, two ghostly figures at a Santa Barbara cemetery, the ghost picture taken at Adelaida Cemetery at "Charlotte's grave" in San Luis Obispo County and the ghost image on the sunken remains of the USS Arizona at Pearl Harbor, Hawaii, complete with Real Audio sound clip.

"Tales From Tombstones" is a wacky collection of Senate's favorite epitaphs, including "Underneath this stone lies poor John Round: Lost at sea and never found!" from a cemetery in Massachusetts.

Like his walking tours of homes of the dead and undead, Senate uses humor throughout his site to keep the Web surfer entertained and educated. And with the country's psyche focused on the search for a witch that never existed, it's fun to have a place to go for information on the apparitions that appear around us every day.

At least according to the ghost stalker.

—**Scott Steepleton**

## SITES TO SEE

SCOTT DRAPER / OUR TIMES

Local ghost chaser Richard Senate leads tours through Ventura City Hall on a Ghosts and Ghould Tour.

# SIXTH SENSE

by Matthew Singer

**Richard Senate sees dead people —**

Richard Senate recalls his first encounter with a ghost the way other people remember the Challenger disaster or the Kennedy assassination. It is one of those profound moments burned so deep in his memory he can summon it with videotaped detail. It was July 3, 1978. He was up late, working on an archaeological dig at Mission San Antonio de Padua in Central California. Around midnight, he left the lab to grab a frozen chicken out of an ice box in the kitchen. On his way there, he noticed a monk shuffling around the courtyard, dressed in a robe and carrying a lit candle. He thought this a bit odd, considering most modern-day monks wear jeans and sweatshirts, but other than that, there didn't appear to be anything out of the ordinary about the guy. When Senate approached to say hello, however, the man literally vanished into the evening air.

At that point, Senate lost his appetite. He went back to his room and tried to sleep, the incident replaying endlessly in his mind. At the time a skeptic of paranormal phenomena, Senate tried to rationalize what he had seen. But no strict scientific explanation made sense. He was sure there had been somebody there; he could even make out the folds of his garment. The next day, he told the mission caretakers about his experience, and they informed him that, oh yes, the place is crawling with phantom monks. The one Senate happened to run into was Brother Joseph, a near-saintly figure during his lifetime who, after his death, continued his nightly ritual of wandering the grounds in prayer. There was no getting around it: Richard Senate had seen a ghost. And it would shape the path of his career for the next three decades.

"People ask me, 'How long after that did you decide to become a ghost hunter?'" he says. His answer: "About thirty seconds."

Since then, Senate has met a lot of spectral beings, many of them in Ventura, the city he has called home for the majority of his 58 years. Although most of his multiple job titles — anthropologist, historian, teacher, author, museum docent, coordinator of historical programming for the City of Ventura — deal with forging an understanding of the natural world, Senate has earned his greatest renown as an explorer of the supernatural. He is credited with creating one of the first Web sites dedicated to ghost hunting and has published 13 books on the subject. He teaches classes on paranormal investigation and leads tours of the county's haunted sites. For Senate, however, the physical and metaphysical are not sovereign states. Knowledge of one can lead to deeper knowledge of the other, and that is ultimately what he is looking for in his exploration of both. His goals are simple; the ramifications are not. "I want to find out what ghosts are — their true nature," he explains. "And the more I delve into it, the more I think there isn't one answer but several, and it's going to go to the essence of reality itself."

Today, Senate is enjoying a three-egg omelet at Nona's Courtyard Café. It was his idea to meet here, and no wonder: the place gives off a spooky vibe only a lover of weird history could appreciate. The restaurant is located inside the Bella Maggiore Inn, a high-end hotel during the oil boom of the 1920s that degenerated into a flophouse before being converted to a bed-and-breakfast in the mid-'70s. To get to the café, you must walk through the hotel lobby, past dangling candelabras and paintings of early 20th century socialites who seem to stare and judge. Nona's itself is vaguely creepy, with its large, European-style courtyard, high retractable ceiling, walls covered in foliage and fountain with a stone lion's head spewing water from its mouth. There's an eerie, antiquated quality about the entire building; even if it was built yesterday, it would probably still be haunted by old spirits.

And indeed it is. According to Senate, around 1940 the body of a prostitute named Sylvia was found hanging in a closet in Room 17. Police ruled it a suicide. But in the ensuing decades, numerous visitors reported strange occurrences happening in the room where she died: lights would flicker; ceiling fans would turn and switch directions by themselves; wallets would disappear; the scent of cheap perfume would suddenly and inexplicably overwhelm the air. Some guests claimed to feel as if they were sharing the bed with an unseen presence, and one woman even testified to being choked after mocking the alleged ghost. Eventually, a séance was held, and Sylvia appeared to proclaim that she did not kill herself but had in fact been murdered by one of her clients, a sailor. She also announced her intention to stay in the hotel until he comes back, to exact a little revenge. Considering the murder happened more than 60 years ago, the chances of a return visit are slim — meaning Sylvia will inhabit Room 17 for a long time to come.

"A bit of advice," Senate offers: "If you check into Room 17, don't sing 'Anchors Aweigh.'"

The story of Sylvia demonstrates one of Senate's favorite proverbs about residents of the netherworld: Ghosts are people, too — "people who just happen to be dead," he says. "Human emotions still apply. The reasons why humans do stuff are the reasons why ghosts do stuff: revenge, love, et cetera." But that awareness still does not fully explain what ghosts actually are. Senate has yet to come to any hard conclusions on that end. He does not, however, subscribe to the notion that all ghosts are formerly flesh-and-blood humans trapped in a state somewhere between life and death. That explanation, promulgated by Hollywood and traditional folklorists, fails to account for why, when people allege to have seen an apparition, a large percentage of them describe someone who is still alive. Ghosts, then, could be the products of time wars, Senate says. Or the manifestation of a kind of psychic energy. Or something else entirely. He isn't

sure. He probably never will be. And he doesn't appear very upset about that. The way he figures it, centuries ago, scientists thought they had the universe figured out; a lot of scientists think the same today. In truth, there are still plenty of unknowns out there, things science, technology and the human brain are not evolved enough to grasp. Hundreds of years from now, who knows? But at this period in time, the answers Senate seeks may just be beyond his, or anyone else's, realm of comprehension.

Of course, that's not going to stop him from searching. Searching, after all, is the common thread linking all of Senate's various occupations. He became fascinated with uncovering the mysteries of the past as a child after watching The Mummy, the 1932 film starring Boris Karloff. In high school, he had the opportunity to participate in an excavation of the district formerly known as Ventura's Chinatown, which led to him majoring in history and anthropology at Cal State Long Beach. Initially, he hoped to teach junior high, but his enthusiasm fizzled once he realized he didn't like any of his fellow teachers. After winding through a series of go-nowhere jobs — sporting goods salesman, clerk at Payless ShoeSource — Senate was hired by the city to be the coordinator of historical programming, a position he kept for 22 years. He ran the Albinger Archaeological Museum as well as the Olivas Adobe Historical Park, where an exhibit hall was named in his honor following his retirement. And he found a way to teach that allowed him to avoid other teachers: through city-sponsored home school programs.

Then, he met Brother Joseph. And that's when he started a search of a different kind.

When Senate joined the ghost hunting community, it was a rarified group. He admits not knowing exactly what he was doing at first, mainly because there were no instruction manuals for how to proceed with such studies. Therefore, he approached his investigations like he would any other archaeological survey, gathering information about a purportedly haunted site, then simply going in and observing. Now, however with the use of the internet, "every kid in a basement with a computer is a ghost hunter." As a result, the field of paranormal research has split into two camps: the scientific ("the nerds," Senate calls them) and the metaphysical, people who wear weird clothes and see ghosts everywhere." Senate places himself somewhere in between. He utilizes instruments such as dowsing rods to gauge supernatural activity,

but in most cases, his most precious tools are still his own eyes and ears.

"In a lot of ways, it's like being a detective," he says. "The goal is to collect information and either prove or disprove the existence of ghosts."

In 1991, Senate began hosting "ghost walks" around Ventura, which he says is "one of the most haunted cities in America." He takes attendees on a tour of the city's particularly spook-infested places, including the Ortega Adobe, the Bard Hospital and city hall, where earlier this year, five people simultaneously witnessed the appearance of the famed "Lady in Red," a woman in '50s garb who supposedly stalks the corridors of the building. Such sightings occur frequently on his tours, Senate says. Once, at the Olivas Adobe, a man openly dared any ghosts that may have been present to make themselves known. Seconds later, an old nightgown on display leapt into the air completely on its own. Naturally, Senate encourages people to bring their cameras.

While the ghost walks have always been popular with tourists and locals, Senate says that interest in the supernatural in general has mushroomed in recent years. He attributes the spike to the return of supernatural themes to popular culture, in movies like The Sixth Sense and The Others and television shows like the Sci Fi Channel's Ghost Hunters. But he also insists there is a broader reason for the public's increasing belief in once-ridiculed theories, one that goes deeper than mere entertainment. "Traditional forces in society are under attack," Senate says. "As such, people are turning to other things for answers. There's a rejection of scientific principles, and the idea of ghosts and things not accepted by science becomes more attractive."

For that reason, the work of Senate and his peers is gradually taking on a significance it never before possessed. If the point of archaeology is to harness the past as a guide to the future, then examining the paranormal is a way to better our understanding of a complicated present. Whether or not we're all seeing dead people isn't the important part; just the fact that we're seeing something is.

"Even if it's all in our heads, it's still worthy of study, to find out why people imagine such things," Senate says. "But the evidence is too powerful. There's more involved than just hallucinations."

*Join Richard Senate for a ghost walk on Oct. 28 or 31. Call 658-4726 for reservations.* ∎

JULY 9, 1999

## Our Psychic World
# Ghostly Lady Haunts Popular Restaurant
### By Richard Senate

The three women didn't expect to meet a ghost when they recently went to dinner at Ventura's Landmark 78 restaurant. They didn't know that a phantom named "Rosa" has been experienced in the old place for a quarter of a century and they were unaware that she haunts the upstairs women's rest room.

That night one of the three witnesses had received a message for "Rosa"! That day she had gone to a psychic in Oxnard and she was told that a spirit had a message, a message he was desperate to have delivered to someone named "Rosa". The message was that "Robert" wanted to meet "Rosa" on "Market Street" and that this was most important. It was a strange message as the women didn't know anyone named "Rosa" and couldn't understand why she was selected to convey this information. She understood later that night. By chance the three friends dinned at the Landmark 78 on Santa Clara Street in Ventura. The restaurant occupies in the historic 1914 Carlo Hain Victorian House, long rumored to have its own distinct ghost. The new owners had heard of the stories and hung framed newspaper clipping of the legend on the wall. During the remodeling of the house some strange things happened, leading them to think that the tales of a ghost might not be simple over-imagination. The three women were stunned to read there was a ghost and chilled when they discovered her name was "Rosa".

As if compelled, the woman with the message went up the long flight of stairs to the second floor bathroom. Her friends were with her to offer "moral support". As they acceded the steps they felt a distinct overpowering coldness that grew stronger with each step. They didn't expect to see

anything in the bathroom, but, as they swept open the door, all three saw a grey figure across the chamber. It was a shadowy form, like moving grey smoke. It had the form of a woman with her hair in a bun, its sleeves puffed and the skirt to the floor in the style of the early part of the century. The specter began to move. The woman with the psychic message quickly stuttered out the words as the figure crossed the room. It walked right though one of the witnesses as it glided across the floor-boards! Then, it vanished into the chilling shadows of the bathroom. Shaken, the three went back to their table, I can only imagine it was to have a stiff drink.

The woman felt relieved that she had given the apparition her message and she hoped that this might put an end to ghostly haunting. The legend of "Rosa" is that she taken her own life after she grew despondent waiting for her lover to return.

Perhaps the spirit called "Robert" was that of the lover, maybe this meeting on Market Street would cause the lovers to unite and release the phantom woman from the house.

The woman hoped this would be the case, sadly, the management tell of other sightings since then. A German family, visiting Ventura, dinned at the Landmark and came away with a lasting impression of the community. The young daughter went up to use the bathroom and when she came down asked their server why there was a lady inside the mirror in the bathroom! Perhaps "Rosa" didn't hear the message or maybe she hasn't forgiven "Robert" for what ever happen so long ago. In researching the ghost story I found that the earliest sighting of the lady was in 1969. Before that no one ever saw a ghost in the old house, in fact they said it was distinctly un-haunted. No one named "Rosa" ever lived in the place and, as far as I could determine, no one had died in the house. Who is "Rosa" and why does she haunt, we do not know, but the stories persist

and the number of people who have encountered this specter grows with each year. What ever she is, it doesn't seem to want to really frighten people. It seems only interested in watching over the place and maybe, continuing her long wait for "Robert".

*If you have felt something on the stairs or in the bathroom of the Landmark 78 on Santa Clara Street Contact this column at my E-Mail address—ghostlamp«Xtags error: Style name too long»*

# The Ghosts of Ventura's City Hall

## By Richard Senate

"If I could guarantee a ghost, I would charge more money for the tour." The line always gets a laugh. I include it at the start of most of my tours. Still, sometimes phantoms do appear on a tour, not often, but enough to keep things interesting. One such event happened recently on a tour of Ventura's historic 1912 City Hall.

The building was constructed in 1912 as the Ventura County Courthouse and Sheriff's Office, and served the county well until they left the lace for larger, and newer structures. The opulent building was saved and converted into the present City Hall for Ventura. It, like many courthouses all over the nation, is rumored to be haunted. I give ghost tours of the building from time to time. This is something I have done for many years, but this was the first time something strange would happen. This was the first time a ghost appeared before members of the tour.

Many of the people who took part in the tour had cameras with them. I encourage people to brings such things in hope they might capture the image of a ghost. Almost from the start, people on the tour began to get round balls of light in their digital cameras. These controversial "orbs" may well be images of ghosts, or other supernatural energy sources, or they might be just flaws in the camera — dust or something else.

I took the group up the wide marble staircase to the second floor Council Chambers. This had once been a courtroom up until 1962. It was here that Ventura's most famous trial was held in 1959 — the murder for hire trial of Elizabeth "Ma" Duncan. I always enjoy telling the story of how she plotted to kill, and succeed in slaying, her daughter-in-law, Olga Duncan. I like to tell the story because some say "Ma" Duncan haunts the room. She was an evil woman in so many ways. More "Orbs" were photographed here. One at the place were the judge would sit, and another one, interestingly, coming out of my head!

Concluding the story, we left the Chambers and went down the hallway to the first floor of the west wing of the building. Some of the group straggled behind. I was at the head to the group and missed what happened. My wife, Debbie, was at the rear of the group and saw it.

As they were approaching the doors to the Community Services Office on the second floor of the west wing, an apparition appeared. It was the image of a woman wearing a red suit and skirt. The thing was also wearing a red hat and high-heeled shoes. Five people saw the specter as it walked towards the double doors and then, reaching out to the doors, vanished away. They never saw the image's face, only her back. From the padded shoulders and seemed stockings she was dressed in the fashions of the Second World War era. From her shoes to her hat, she was all in red. Debbie caught a psychic impression that the woman was in a hurry and angry about something. Long ago these offices housed the Ventura County Sheriff's Office. From the styling and rich color of the suit this was a well-dressed woman, perhaps a business woman or lawyer. The ghost was seen for just a few seconds before it abruptly vanished. This stunned group was almost speechless at the sighting. Interestingly, they were far from the first to see the ghost. She has been seen off and on since the late 1950s. She is not only seen but heard, as the invisible clicking of high heels on the floor. The last sightings was in May of 1990 and June of 1994. The witnesses all agree on one point; she is short. They said she was no more than a little over five feet tall. This might explain why she was wearing two-inch heels. Using Debbie's help I managed to draw a simple picture of the ghost for my files. I wondered if she would she appear to another group of tourists?

Weeks later I was set to lead another nighttime ghost tour of the historic city hall building. I was hoping that lightning would strike twice, and the mysterious Lady in Red would appear to this new group. I told them of the ghost and we tried several experiments attempting to attract the phantom but to no avail. We went back to the council chambers were I once again told them the stories of "Ma" Duncan.

As we were to leave with the second group, another strange thing happened. This time we all saw it. The room is now used for City Council meetings, and so a long desk dominates one end of the room. Here is where the Councilmen and Councilwomen and the Mayor sit. The high-backed chairs were neatly arranged at the desk, at least they were when we walked into the chambers. One of the group on the tour pointed out that two of the chairs had moved. I stopped talking as everyone looked at the long desk.

As I tried to discount the movement as perhaps caused by vibrations from the street, the two chairs began to move more dramatically. Then a third chair began to pivot and move almost as if pulled by invisible hands. One of the group began to feel an icy presence in the room that sent violent chills down her back. Was this the ghost of "Ma" Duncan? Or maybe a phantom city council was preparing for a late night meeting of some sort? We left the ghosts to what ever they were up to, and continued the tour.

Two different groups, two different dates, yet they both witnessed strange inexpiable events. In all of my years giving tours at the old city hall building nothing like this has ever happened before. Other sites, yes, but not here in the marble halls of this historic structure. I am looking forward to new tours of the place coming in the next few weeks.

*Richard Senate, Oak View*

# Life/style

# Halloween perfect time

## Hunter of spooks scares up eyewitness accounts of

**By JILL BOEKENOOGEN**
Press-Courier Staff Writer

Oxnard is a haunted place.

Or at least people report seeing ghosts in and around the city in private homes, businesses and even cruising the streets.

Ghost hunter and Camarillo resident Richard Senate has been collecting the stories of specters and hauntings for more than a decade. Without judging as to their validity, he interviews the people who have seen the apparition and inspects the area of sighting.

Although he reported never hearing of a Halloween experience, Senate would be available the day after to hear about any encounters with the spirits. The ghost-tale gatherer said Halloween began as a Celtic observance when the dead were believed to return to their homes.

**SENATE MAKES** it clear he is not a parapsychologist. He is the site manager for Ventura's Albinger Archaeological Museum and the Olivas Adobe. His job at the adobe is handy for his passion since "a lot of ghosts hang out, out there." He holds a degree in anthropology and was a teacher in secondary school following his graduation from California State University at Long Beach.

It was when he was participating in an archaeological study in 1978 in King City, that he saw his first ghost, he said. Following his first sighting, he began "collecting ghost stories and evaluating ghost stories," said Senate.

He has also authored "Ghosts of Ventura County" and "Ghosts of the Haunted Coast."

One of the first stories he heard about Oxnard was a head which floated near the corner of C Street and Gonzales Road. Senate added he has heard of a couple of sightings of the head which is supposed to float about five feet above the ground. Senate said he was told the ghost was of a man who was decapitated and is seeking his murderer, but added, "that is purely speculation."

Another ghost which Senate investigated was the report of a haunting of a former bank building in Oxnard. Bank employees reported hearing screams, the tinkling of bells and rapping inside the building. They also reported having the feeling of being watched and seeing a form in the rear of the building.

Senate said he spent about a month investigating the apparition, including a session with a Ouija board and a physic. Information came to Senate that a woman was supposed to have been murdered Dec. 28, 1917, by her husband.

'Anywhere men undergo stress and die, ghosts can be found.'

—Richard Senate

"THIS IS one of my earliest cases," said the ghost hunter. "One of the first stories I ever heard."

Senate heard the tale in early 1979. A woman getting out of her car after a trip to the market saw what she thought at first was a balloon floating above the street. She reported that on a closer look it was the decapitated head of a man with a mustache. Senate's written account of the incident ends with the notation that the woman dropped her groceries when she saw the head.

"I don't know anything other than that," he said.

HOWEVER, HE found no evidence that such a person or event ever took place at the site, said Senate. A check of the newspapers around that date, reveal no such account.

The experience at the bank did hold one surprise for Senate. He saw the spirit.

According to Senate, he was near the back staircase (and at the end of his investigation), when he saw what looked like a figure of white mist coming up the stairs toward him.

"I don't see a lot of ghosts," he said.

Night security guards from an Oxnard hotel reported seeing several apparitions in the hotel, including

# to tell ghost tales
## of hauntings of homes, businesses, streets

a horse on the second floor and a Chinese man in one room. Senate said he investigated the sighting in July, 1984.

"I think we're looking through the fabric of time and seeing the images of past or future event," he said. An explanation for the horse on the second floor is at some future time a rowdy conventioneer may bring a horse up the elevator, he said.

PORT HUENEME has its share of specters. One is a haunted hamburger stand, now a taco place, which Senate visited in 1983. At that time, employees noted having strange feelings, and of doors opening on their own. Senate said during construction, bones and tombstones were uncovered at the site. Nothing strange was reported by the ghost hunter.

The current manager of the fast-food outlet said he has had no experiences with any spooks.

A number of homes have been reported as having additional occupants. One such house is on F street, which Senate said he checked into in May of 1986. The occupants reported hearing footsteps at night, moving curtains, and cold spots in rooms and rushes of air. Other reports of homes in Oxnard being haunted included hearing rapping and feeling cold spots in rooms.

A SILVER Strand Beach home is reportedly haunted. Senate said the owner, who then lived in the building, reported to him in February 1983, that she saw a spirit walk by a window. She also reported that it appeared the ghost was watching her while she was in the bathroom. Senate said it was reported to him the house was used by Rudolph Valentino while he stayed in the area filming "The Sheik." The owner no longer lives in the residence, but rents it out.

When people come to Senate with their ghost stories, he says he listens.

"A lot appear to be panicky," he said, adding that some of the apparitions have down-to-earth answers.

"A lot of cases it's hysteria," Senate said. "They get real jumpy. I try to calm them down and relieve their fears."

However, Senate said he recognizes that everything cannot be logically explained away.

"GHOSTS DO exist, but not like the stories on TV. They may just be images of the past. We don't know what ghosts are. Spirits of the dead. Shadows of the past," he said. "Most are completely harmless or even friendly."

The ghost hunter quoted polls which said 10 percent of the population has seen a ghost, if that holds true, 6,000 in Oxnard can be included.

One factor in the widespread haunting of the area is ghosts manifest themselves in areas of cultural conflict and diversity, he said.

"Let's face it, Oxnard is culturally diversified," he said.

Ghosts do tend to pop up anywhere where people have died under stress — prisons, hospitals, battlefields — he said.

"ANYWHERE men undergo stress and die, ghosts can be found," said Senate.

He suggested one explanation as to why some people may see a spirit and others do not. One theory holds that ghosts are not seen with the eyes, but with the brain.

"It depends on the frame of mind on why one person will see and another does not," he said. "That's one theory."

According to Senate, the people who believe in ghosts are more likely to see them, but "if unbelievers do see ghosts, they will become believers."

# SHOCKING PSYCHIC SOLUTION:

June 29, 2007 • Issue Number 447

## OUR PSYCHIC WORLD
## The Black Dog of Death: My First Ghost Hunt
### By Richard Senate

When I was growing up in the Conejo Valley in the late 1950s, there was a sort of rumor, or legend that circulated in the legend that circulated in the schoolyard of Conejo Elementary School. Maybe it was just a story, but I must credit the yarn for my early interests in ghosts and the supernatural. It was the story of the Black Dog of Death. According to the tale there was a huge black ghost dog that wandered about the Conejo Valley, and anyone unlucky enough to see the creature would die within the month. One unfortunate student had tragically died suddenly of cancer, and the rumor was he had encountered the dog one afternoon. I do not believe the story was true, but it was believed by a good many of the students.

It was rather fun, in a cruel sort of way. You could approach a group of younger students, point and say, "Look, there is the Black Dog of Death! Can't you see it? It's coming this way." The kids would shield their eyes and run away in terror. As the weeks passed, the story evolved somewhat. The supernatural hound was said to live in the old pioneer cemetery on the eastern end of the town. The place looked like some western "Boot Hill" with wooden fences, headstones at strange angles and lots of weeds. It looked like a set for a horror movie and, for all I know, it may have been used for one a time or two. The dog haunted the grave of a man who was believed to be the meanest man in the valley, and had one of the largest stones in the graveyard. The Ghost Dog would appear at exactly 11:42 each night before it prowled the valley. Now, why that time and not midnight? I haven't a guess, except it may have sounded cooler than midnight.

In truth, I didn't believe in the legendary Black Dog. But my friend and I decided to investigate by spending the night next to the grave and watching for the infamous Death Dog. I don't know why we did this, maybe it was something that would only excite a 12-year-old boy. So we did it. I told my folks I was spending the night with my friend (only partly a lie), and he told his that he was spending the night with me. We got our sleeping bags and a few supplies, and we were off to the old cemetery. We brought flashlights, a portable radio, some soft drinks and some snacks. We also had a camera with a flash unit to take a picture of the infamous dog if it did appear. Looking back, we had more courage than brains.

The place had high weeds so no one could see us from the roads or far-away houses. The fence had several holes large enough to drive a car through, so access wasn't a problem. Remember, this was another time, another age, when most people were ready to let boys be boys. We set up our camp next to the large stone monument and talked, listened to the radio, and joked around like kids do. We saw the sun go down turning the sky gold and lifting the oppressive heat of the valley. We drank our drinks and feasted on our snacks as we joked about how we would spend our last month alive – if the death dog really did come.

It got cold quick and we snuggled into our sleeping bags as the stars came out over us. Now the talk of ghosts began to take on a new life. Back in the days when Thousand Oaks really had 1000 oaks there were few street lights. The darkness was inky black. The hours passed slowly as we exhausted any and all topics of conversation, and began to think we should have included a deck of cards with our supplies. We kept watch on the time, and as the magic moment of 11:42 approached my heart began to race. Just as the watch hit 11:40 we heard a sound in the weeds. It was something like an animal approaching!

My heart leaped into my throat as I scanned the underbrush. In my mind's eye, I imagined the huge black dog ready to rip us apart for our disbelief. My hand was on the flashlight and I snapped it on, pointing the beam into the grass. Two red eyes flashed back at me, moved and ran away with great bounds. It was a large jack rabbit! Then they were then found all over the valley (conejo is Spanish for "rabbit" after all). My friend and I laughed and laughed for 20 minutes. By 1:00 a.m. we were asleep, and our night was uninterrupted by ghosts or demon dogs. It was my first ghost hunt, and it was a bust. Still it did confirm that the story of the Black Dog haunting the cemetery was just so much folklore. The cemetery is gone now, and the graves relocated. But, I still wonder if the story of the Black Dog of Death is told in Conejo Valley.

*Richard Senate, Oak View*

# Do You Live in a Haunted House?

### by Richard Senate

## *Here's a test to find out whether to call Ghost Busters*

For anyone who lives in a haunted place there comes a time when the evidence of your own eyes is too much to ignore. It is then that the idea that you live in a haunted house becomes a recognized fact. You can scoff and give brave, rational answers to the strange and unexplainable events that are happening all around you for only so long. These excuses become all the more strained as time passes. At last you feel there can be no other explanation than a ghost (or ghosts).

At that time one should try to call in an expert. Ghost hunters and such are, in some small way, akin to plumbers. Just as you attempt to fix your own pipes at your peril so it is with having a specter lodging with you. It may well be cheaper to "do it yourself," but this can also be unwise.

So, I have devised a simple test for you to take if you believe that you may be living in, or working in, a haunted site.

| | | |
|---|---|---|
| 1. Have you ever heard a voice in this location when there was no one there? | Yes | No |
| 2. Has the TV or computer turned itself on by itself? | Yes | No |
| 3. Have you seen doors open and close by themselves without a reason? | Yes | No |
| 4. At any time, have you smelled something out of the ordinary? | Yes | No |
| 5. Have you ever had things vanish only to turn up a few days later? | Yes | No |
| 6. Have you ever seen any object move on its own, without reason? | Yes | No |
| 7. Have you ever awakened from a sound sleep certain that there had been a scream? | Yes | No |
| 8. Do you find one part of the building strangely cold when it should not be? | Yes | No |
| 9. Do you ever feel "watched" in the bathroom? | Yes | No |
| 10. Are there any odd stains in the building that look like blood? | Yes | No |
| 11. Do animals, such as dogs and cats, avoid rooms in the structure? | Yes | No |
| 12. Do small children scream when forced to enter a room in the building? | Yes | No |
| 13. Has there ever been a murder or suicide in the structure? | Yes | No |
| 14. Was there ever a battle fought near the site? | Yes | No |
| 15. Have you ever found Native American artifacts near the location? | Yes | No |
| 16. Do you have persistent nightmares when you stay at the structure? | Yes | No |
| 17. Have you ever, out of the corner of your eye, seen a "shadow" move at the site? | Yes | No |
| 18. Have you ever felt something invisible touch you at the site? | Yes | No |
| 19. Have you ever gotten a white spot or shaft in pictures taken at the site? | Yes | No. |
| 20. Do creative people seem disturbed being in the building? | Yes | No. |
| 21. Have you had pictures, crosses, etc. fall off the walls by themselves? | Yes | No |
| 22. Do fireplace fires or candles act oddly in the house? | Yes | No |
| 23. Have you ever seen odd markings appear on the walls, such as "Get Out"? | Yes | No |
| 24. Does the bathroom toilet flush itself? | Yes | No. |

If you answered "yes" to at least ten of these questions, you live or work in a haunted site. If you answered "yes" to five of them, it is possible that you live or work in a haunted building. If you answered "yes" to 15 or more, you should seek help and advice as soon as possible! For more information contact me via e-mail at ghostlamp@msn.com.

# INNER LIGHT / GLOBAL COMMUNICATIONS
## EXPLORING THE WORLD'S GREATEST MYSTERIES SINCE 1965

DISTRIBUTED BY GLOBAL COMMUNICATIONS

**ORDER ALL TITLES FROM GLOBAL COMMUNICATIONS**

**GLOBAL COMMUNICATIONS**
Post Office Box 753
New Brunswick, New Jersey 08903

FOR OVER 40 YEARS Inner Light / Global Communications has brought to the world some of the best authors on Mysticism, Metaphysics, and the Unexplained. Our best recognized authors include: John A. Keel; Brad Steiger; Commander X; T. Lobsang Rampa; Tim Swartz; Timothy Green Beckley; William Alexander Oribello and Dragonstar.

## OUR NUMBER ONE BEST SELLER!
## OVER 50,000 COPIES IN PRINT!

**THE LOST JOURNALS OF NIKOLA TESLA: HAARP—CHEMTRAILS AND THE SECRET OF ALTERNATIVE 4** by Tim Swartz

Discredited in his time, Nikola Tesla was made out by business competitors and the government to be nothing more than a crackpot. Nonetheless, these same conspirators later duplicated, and possibly even stole, many of Tesla's most famous inventions. Here is sensational data obtained from the inventor's most private papers and kept under wraps by military and big business concerns. Many of Tesla's most powerful and potentially dangerous scientific discoveries are being turned against ordinary citizens in programs of behavior and physical modification, including the seeding of clouds with mind and body altering chemicals. This book explores reverse gravity, free energy, contact with hidden dimensions, mysterious radio signals from space, earth changes, freak weather patterns, electric death rays, UFOs and particle beam weapons. ISBN: 1-892062-13-5 • $15.95

**OTHER TESLA TITLES INCLUDE:**
**NIKOLA TESLA: FREE ENERGY AND THE WHITE DOVE** by Commander X

Top Secret revelations by a former military intelligence operative regarding Tesla's secret propulsion system and how the Secret Government is flying anti-gravity craft. Reveals Tesla's "Cosmic Roots," and the existence of a remote underground site in Nevada where these craft are being hangared. ISBN: 0-938284-82-2 • $15.00

**NIKOLA TESLA'S JOURNEY TO MARS—ARE WE ALREADY THERE?** by Sean Casteel

Jules Verne wrote what was at the time considered to be far-fetched stories about the exploration of the moon and Mars. These classic literary works were based upon "wild rumors" circulating that such voyages had already occurred, with a group of scientists, all members of the same secret society. They had tapped into an unknown power source, using it to usher in the birth of flight years before the Wright Brothers flew their plane at Kittyhawk. Stranger than any fiction book could be, here is proof the NAZIs established colonies on the moon in the early 1940s; facts NASA doesn't want you to know! ISBN: 1-892062-31-3 • $14.95

**INVISIBILITY AND LEVITATION—HOW-TO KEYS TO PERSONAL PERFORMANCE** by Commander X—Utilized by occultists and the martial arts, these are not parlor tricks, but actual methods adopted by the ancients and now used by the military intelligence community to perfect invisibility as demonstrated during the Philadelphia Experiment and Stealth Technology. This book offers various techniques that really work, providing the reader with dozens of examples which takes the subject out of its mystical surroundings. ISBN: 0-938294-36-9 • $15.95

CONTINUED ON NEXT PAGE >